D0262013

DISASTERS AND THE MEDIA
Managing crisis communications

DISASTERS AND THE MEDIA

Managing crisis communications

Edited by

SHIRLEY HARRISON

Foreword by George Howarth

MACMILLAN
Business

First published 1999 by
MACMILLAN PRESS LTD
Houndmills, Basingstoke, Hampshire RG21 6XS
and London
Companies and representatives
throughout the world

ISBN 0–333–71785–6

A catalogue record for this book is available
from the British Library.

This book is printed on paper suitable for recycling and
made from fully managed and sustained forest sources.

10 9 8 7 6 5 4 3 2 1
08 07 06 05 04 03 02 01 00 99

Printed in Great Britain by
Antony Rowe Ltd
Chippenham, Wiltshire

For Rob
with love and gratitude

CONTENTS

LIST OF TABLES

LIST OF FIGURES

LIST OF EXHIBITS

FOREWORD

Disasters, crises and emergencies can strike suddenly and unexpectedly, anywhere and at any time. The causes may be sudden and unpredictable. One factor, however, is certain. The news media will be close behind.

Many agencies have a part in dealing with disaster and its aftermath. The emergency services, voluntary organisations, hospitals, local authorities, central government departments and companies may all be involved. But the media are always major players, for good or ill. In the provision of information to the public, they can be an invaluable ally.

This book draws on the experience of experts to disseminate good practice in dealing with the media and public information at a time of disaster. Lessons which have been learned – by the media, the emergency services, local authorities and others – from the Hillsborough disaster and the Dunblane tragedy are presented here with the aim of improving relations between the media and organisations concerned with disaster. With advanced planning and a better understanding of each other's role, the response to a disaster can be improved, and the trauma caused to those caught up in the process can be reduced.

I commend this book to you.

George Howarth
Permanent Under Secretary of State
Home Office

PREFACE

The subject matter

Crisis management is of increasing importance to organisations. In a time of single-issue pressure groups, footloose consumers and tactical voters, no body in either the public or the private sector can afford to neglect preparation for dealing with the crises, disasters and emergencies in which it may become embroiled. Hence this book will be of interest to all those concerned with the management of organisations.

Crises, disasters and emergencies are, and always have been, newsworthy. The stereotypical Shock! Horror! headline has become shorthand for disaster reporting, which sells more papers. Those in the media, or wanting to be, will find contributors in this book giving the view from the studio, the news-room and behind the camera.

The potential for misinformation in crises and disasters is immense. Just at the time when good communication is vital, it falls apart. Hence professional communicators – those responsible for public relations and the provision of public information – will be interested in the insights offered in this book.

You – the reader

This book is intended primarily for managers and would-be managers in all fields of business and the public sector, who will be able to make practical use of the chapters demonstrating good practice in a number of fields. Those working in the media, in the emergency services and in public policy areas will find their experiences reflected in this book and will also find the extended case study on the Hillsborough disaster to be of value for the lessons it provides.

Management, business, media, communication and public relations specialists will benefit additionally from studying the issues raised in Part I of the book. In the current climate, which is, in my view rightly, holding organisations more to account for their behaviour, reputations will be earned and kept on the basis of that behaviour. At a time of crisis or disaster, organisational behaviour is under the spotlight.

The book should also prove useful as supplementary reading for those studying relevant subjects: management and business, journalism and media studies, public relations and corporate communications, both at undergraduate and postgraduate level.

The book

This book aims to help managers and potential managers to understand the importance of planning for crisis management, by raising awareness of the effect of disasters and crises on the organisations concerned, their stakeholders, the media and the public at large. It aims to improve the relationship between the media and those subject to media scrutiny by generating mutual understanding of their needs. Drawing on the experience of practitioners it aims to disseminate good practice.

A number of books have been published, mostly in the United States, which cover related topics in the fields of the media reporting of disasters, crisis public relations and disaster preparedness. Some disasters, such as Lockerbie, Bhopal and the Exxon *Valdez*, have generated their own literature: an extensive bibliography is provided at the end of this book. However, none of those books takes the approach of bringing together the major players in the drama of a crisis: the organisations affected, the emergency services, public relations professionals and the media.

The book is made up of four sections. Part I sets the context and raises some general issues on the theme of communicating at a time of crisis or disaster.

Part II looks at relationships between the media and those who are trying to manage the crisis in public relations and public information terms. It explains how the different media work, what their needs are, and how they can become allies or foes. This section contains a number of case studies, each contributed by an expert in his or her field, which clearly explain how a variety of crises and disasters were managed by the organisations concerned, and how they were reported by the media.

Part III is an extended case study of the Hillsborough disaster, taking a candid look at what happened from the perspective of four very different people who were closely involved in the aftermath.

The final section includes chapters on the value of training and rehearsal, and some of the hard-won lessons learned on dealing with the media at major disasters in the past, including Dunblane.

Acknowledgements

This book would not have been written without the inspiration, support and advice of a large number of people, among them fellow media and public relations professionals, emergency planners, colleagues in the academic world and those whose research I have supervised. There are too many to list here – but they know who they are. Between them they demonstrated the need, gave me ideas, provided material, helped me to find things out, and acted as a sounding board for my thoughts. To them all – thank you. Thanks also to the Emergency Planning College, and to the respective editors of the Sheffield *Star* and the Liverpool *Echo* for permission to reproduce copyright material.

I must single out a few people for special thanks. My ineptitude as an editor has been covered up by the skill of the contributors, who have made the writing of this book a social pleasure as well as an intellectual endeavour: Clive Ferguson, Mike Granatt, Alf Green, Tom Hardie-Forsyth, Peter Hayes, John Jefferson, Paddy Marley, Peter Whitbread (and Denise Vaughan), and Peter Young. Thanks also to George Howarth for contributing the Foreword; to Alan Underwood, who brought many of us together in the first place; to Ian Hampton, John Parkinson and Tom Picton-Phillipps for their good humour and invaluable help; to Sam Whittaker at Macmillan for her advice and encouragement; and to Jacob Harrison, who patiently waited a long time for the computer. Finally, thanks to Rob Harrison, my partner in this as in so many other endeavours, and on whom I can always rely to make everything work, even the software.

Shirley Harrison
September 1997

NOTES ON THE CONTRIBUTORS

Peter Young

After graduating from Gonville and Caius College, Cambridge, Peter Young worked in public relations before becoming an independent writer in 1976. He has written articles on computers, communications and management subjects; and business histories, including the centenary history of Standard Telephones and Cables, *Power of Speech* (1983) and *Mutuality, The Story of the UK P & I Club* (1995). He is currently researching the history of the insurance company General Accident. *Disasters: focusing on management responsibility* was published in 1993 by the Herald Charitable Trust.

Shirley Harrison

Shirley Harrison has worked for 20 years in the communications industry and is a member of the National Union of Journalists, an active member of the Institute of Public Relations (sitting on its Local Government Group Management Committee) and a former in-house director of public relations. She lectures widely at undergraduate, postgraduate and professional level, while continuing to work as an independent researcher and consultant. She is the author of the standard text *Public Relations: An Introduction* (1995) and has had published numerous chapters and journal articles on public policy, business ethics, corporate communications and crisis management.

Clive Ferguson

As Home Assignment Editor for BBC TV news, Clive Ferguson deploys crews, correspondents and resources on both diary and breaking stories. Having graduated from Trinity College, Dublin, he began working for the BBC in Northern Ireland, on radio and television news. He produced and presented the local programme *Scene around Six* before moving in 1981 to London as a reporter for television news. He covered military coups, the Falklands War (from

Buenos Aires), disasters, emergencies, crashes and sieges from all over the globe before taking up his present position in 1990.

Peter Whitbread

Peter Whitbread has spent most of his career within the Government Information Service, working in press, exhibitions and displays and a variety of management roles including training. In his post as director of the Central Office of Information for the south west region he deals with all chief emergency planning officers in the region and has attended many emergency exercises. He has also worked for the Employment Service, the Training, Enterprise and Education Directorate, Health and Safety Executive and ACAS.

John Jefferson

John Jefferson began his journalistic career on the Bridlington *Free Press* and Scarborough *Evening News* before joining Thomson Newspapers in the north east. His BBC career as a reporter and producer took him to BBC Radios Durham, Teesside and Carlisle and Radio 4's *Today* programme. He was programme organiser at Radio Humberside before launching Radio York as station manager. He was managing editor of BBC Radio Leeds for six years and was a member of the BBC's 10-year strategy team before retiring in 1996.

Tom Hardie-Forsyth

Now a course director at the Emergency Planning College, Tom Hardie-Forsyth originally trained as a marine communications officer and electronics engineer. He was Military Liaison Officer to the Foreign Office Overseas Development Administration's Response Team during Operation Safe Haven in northern Iraq in 1991.

Michael Granatt

Michael Granatt is Director, Communication, at the Home Office. He has held equivalent posts at the Departments of Environment and Energy, and the Metropolitan Police. His experience, on which he has lectured widely, includes the *Marchioness* disaster, Piper Alpha, the hurricane of October 1987, and Chernobyl. He is Director of the Government Information Service.

Alf Green

Alf Green spent 50 years with regional newspapers until his retirement as news editor of the Liverpool *Echo* in 1993. In that time he covered a number of major disasters, ranging from Aberfan to the Heysel and Hillsborough Stadium disasters. He was awarded the MBE in 1994 for his services to journalism.

Paddy Marley

Paddy Marley, now retired, worked for Liverpool City Council for more than 30 years. In 1985 he became assistant director (administration) in the social services department where he was responsible for all personnel, finance, transport and general administration. This appointment led to his close involvement in Liverpool Council's response to the Hillsborough tragedy.

Peter Hayes

Peter Hayes has a law degree, a master's degree in the study of organisations and was awarded the Queen's Police Medal for his work in improving the organisational health and welfare facilities available to the police. He was a police officer for 36 years and retired as Deputy Chief Constable of South Yorkshire Police in 1993. The majority of his police experience was operational and he was involved with a number of major incidents, including the Hillsborough disaster.

PART I

PERSPECTIVES

PERSPECTIVES

How the news media cover crises, disasters and civil emergencies is the basis for this book. As some of the contributors explain, there are no clear dividing lines to be drawn between what a crisis, disaster or emergency is. In a crisis a company's reputation may be at risk or there may be a crisis of confidence in the company's products or its management. In a disaster there will be loss of life or property, injury or trauma on a relatively large scale. A civil emergency will involve one or more of the emergency or so-called 'blue light' services and possibly local or central government, and their response to it may prevent the emergency's escalating into a disaster.

However such events and incidents are defined, there is one thing they have in common. They are all news. Terrible events, the fall of the mighty, shock and horror are the essence of hard news. They sell newspapers; they deliver viewers and listeners. Communication at a time of crisis or disaster is a necessity.

This part of the book aims to set the context and to raise some general issues on the theme of communicating at a time of crisis or disaster. In Chapter 1, Peter Young shows how organisations have failed to learn from previous disasters, and how history has repeated itself. He places the responsibility firmly at the door of managers. Chapter 2 looks at the main issues surrounding management responsibility and how communicating is integral to them all: to the management of reputation, to preparedness, and to training and rehearsal.

Real crises, disasters and emergencies are not about issues, however. They are, usually, about people. So it may be helpful to look back ten years or so, to remind ourselves of some of the disasters which have occurred, and the scale of the problem which we are looking at in this book.

The latter half of the 1980s was a period of disasters in the UK. Some of the major incidents are shown in Table 1.

The death toll is by no means the whole sad story. In far greater number, victims remain. Survivors, the apparently lucky ones, often take longer to recover from the psychological than the physical effects. As well as repairing shattered lives bereaved relatives usually face a long legal battle to establish responsibility for a particular disaster. Unless they are represented by a trade union or other organisation, everything they do is a cost and recovering it is problematical.

Companies, on the other hand, pass on responsibility for paying out to their insurers. In any case, managements can more easily afford the expense and time of going to court, charging the outgoings against the company and regarding a fine as no more than a cost of doing business.

Date	Incident	Deaths
6 May 1985	Bradford, football stand fire	56
6 March 1987	Zeebrugge, *Herald of Free Enterprise* sinking	193
19 August 1987	Hungerford, shooting massacre	16
18 November 1987	King's Cross, escalator fire	31
1988 (9 days)	Grangemouth, BP refinery explosions	3
6 July 1988	North Sea, Piper Alpha platform fire	167
12 December 1988	Clapham Junction, 3-train crash	35
21 December 1988	Lockerbie, Pan Am Flight 103 crash	270
8 January 1989	M1, British Midland Boeing 737 crash	50
4 March 1989	Purley, rail crash	5
15 April 1989	Hillsborough Stadium, crush	96
20 August 1989	River Thames, boat collision and sinking	57

Table 1 Disasters of the 1980s
Source: Emergency Planning College

It can even be shown that disasters are good for business. Where a company can show that it has coped well with a disaster, learned the lessons and taken steps to ensure such an event does not happen again, the share price is likely to rise (Buckingham 1997). For example, British Midland increased its market share on the London--Belfast route following the M1 crash, and Commercial Union's share price had increased by 22 per cent six months after its headquarters was blown apart by the Baltic Exchange bomb.

But where a company's management is considered to have performed badly, either in the period leading up to the incident or in dealing with the aftermath, the reverse happens. Exxon's shares had fallen by 18 per cent six months after the *Valdez* environmental disaster, and Union Carbide's by almost a third after the Bhopal tragedy (*ibid.*).

Purely in terms of good business, then, planning for a crisis or disaster, and how to deal with the communication issues arising from such an event, are the right things to do. The two chapters that follow expand on this theme.

Reference

Buckingham, L. (1997) 'Dead customers do not have to hurt share price' *Guardian* 1 March

1 THE CONTEXT

Peter Young

The early 1990s have been lean years. They started in economic recession and the recovery has been marked by cuts: downsizing of organisations, with losses concentrated among middle management, leaving fewer experienced staff to do more; and cuts in budgets to get greater value for money but not always providing resources adequate for the tasks to be performed. In theory, organisations are tighter, flatter, more efficient, with a sharper performance, revealed on the bottom line.

Figures do not tell the whole story. Managers often feel they are barely keeping pace while looking over their shoulders for the next wave of cuts, possibly redundancy, which may bear no relationship to their own performance. They are caught in the pincers of technological change and the relentless demands of the bottom line.

In these circumstances there is a smaller margin for error and coping with the unforeseen, which does not bode well for either the likelihood of disasters occurring or any handling of them. For example, fire service personnel are fewer and hospital beds, especially for intensive care, are rarely empty. On the face of it, this is a recipe for disaster. Yet, mercifully, so far in the 1990s the United Kingdom has been spared the clusters of disasters that happened in the latter half of the 1980s – the enterprising decade when everyone was making money. In the pursuit of profit, safety came on the debit side of the account. Even minor expenses such as clearing combustible litter from under a football stand or fitting a light on the bridge of a ferry indicating that bow doors were closed before sailing were ignored. Procedures were allowed to become sloppy.

The relative absence of disasters in the 1990s might suggest that lessons have been learned. That would be a rash claim. The pressures on business are even greater and there are priorities above safety on the agenda. As the frontiers of the state have been rolled back and cuts made in public expenditure, society expects more of business. Private industry is expected to make many of the provisions in community involvement, education, sponsorship of arts and sport that were formerly a public responsibility. At the same time, through consumer pressures and legislation, society demands a greater accountability from business in its impact on the environment, its use of energy, its concern for customers and its moral attitudes shown in how and where it does business. To an organisation these are pressing everyday concerns whereas a disaster is something that just might happen. While it is seen to be sensible to have a contingency plan against such an event so that any crisis can be managed, so often the concern of the organisation is more for the harm that might be done to its reputation than the effects of the event upon the individuals involved. Loss of capital seems to take priority over the loss of human life and commercial considerations come before the human, to the point where the organisation is legally blameless.

Even though people have died, nobody seems to be responsible in law. For example in the Zeebrugge case a coroner's jury found that 187 victims had been unlawfully killed, whereas at the Central Criminal Court three years later a judge directed his jury to return a verdict that nobody was guilty of unlawful killing. At the criminal trial defence counsel maintained that none of the ferry company's senior personnel could be found guilty of manslaughter because there was no evidence that any of them had been made aware of the risk of a ferry sailing with its bow doors open. The prosecution insisted that men of their standing and experience ought to have been aware of it. Regrettably, that issue was discounted.

To the public, sophisticated legal arguments often seem to get in the way of common sense. A company has a liability for its products and consumers have rights but when it comes to the question of corporate responsibility in disasters the situation is unsatisfactory, doubly unsatisfactory. For each group of victims it presents an opportunity to establish responsibility, after expensive and lengthy voluntary effort often ending in disappointment. For organisations it means a reduction of external discipline, the greater chance of being found guilty of a lesser offence.

As so often the law lags behind events. In our mass society, seen in vast crowds, large transport and distribution systems, grand-scale engineering and construction projects, the consequences of accidents, however simple, are magnified. Some disasters respect no frontiers.

For instance, radioactivity from the 1986 explosion at Chernobyl in the Ukraine, borne by the wind, affected Welsh sheep and Lapland reindeer pastures for years later. The long-term effects were greater and wider than the immediate 31 deaths.

Moreover, the overall situation is not static. The pace of change in society and technology is accelerating, with the nature and content of people's jobs altering as frequently as every five years. Yet the definition of corporate responsibility has not kept pace with these developments. Survivors of disasters and their relatives are still fighting for the situation to be properly recognised and the law to follow suit.

For all these reasons one must be sceptical about the lessons of the 1980s having been learned. On a long view managements do not learn from history as much as they might. They live, don't learn and let die. The extent of the accident problem is probably understated. Statistics, except in the event of known deaths and injuries, are often incomplete. For the sake of a quiet life, not all incidents are reported and near-misses are widely ignored. They become significant only later, when the reality of hazards is apparent. All too often there is an assumption of safety, a failure to recognise that old policies and procedures are no longer adequate to a new situation. That is the 'horseless carriage' approach. There is also the comfort of the false logic that because something has not happened so far it will not happen.

The potential for disaster

A common feature of disasters is that in hindsight they could have been avoided. For many of them occur either where there is a high risk, not just in recognised hazardous industries, or a historical precedent. Each disaster, no matter in what industry, ought to be an occasion for a reassessment of risks elsewhere, not a self-congratulatory sigh of relief that it has happened to somebody else. A disaster is essentially the failure of a system, a terrible example to others that their own system needs thorough re-examination. An impression of a low degree of risk can be reinforced by a search for the immediate cause, which often turns out to be apparently minor. A quick fix is not the answer. The whole system has to be overhauled and hindsight turned into foresight.

An obvious point is that the density of population and the amount of activity in an area increase the potential for disaster.

The fire on 18 November 1987 at King's Cross, killing 31 people, occurred on a wooden escalator at the busiest station on the London Underground network, used by some 250,000 travellers a day. Faulty weekend overtime work on a new signalling system caused the crash of three trains, the death of 35 people and injuries to some 200 others on 12 December 1988 at Clapham Junction. In World War Two parlance both places were 'vulnerable points'. There is much to be said for establishing hazard ratings for places and operations, as the chemical industry has for the transport of its various materials or insurers do when granting cover.

Any concentration of people, as at football grounds, increases risks. Examples are

Ibrox Park, Glasgow, where 66 fans were crushed and over 140 injured on 2 January 1971 when, on an equalising goal being scored near the end of a Rangers v. Celtic match, fans surged forward, breaking down crash barriers. Crash barriers had collapsed 10 years earlier, also during a Rangers v. Celtic match, on 16 September 1961, when two people were killed and several injured.

Heysel Stadium in the final of the European Cup on 29 May 1985 when, following violent crowd disturbances and the collapse of a side wall, 39 spectators died and some 400 were injured.

Hillsborough Stadium, where 95 people, mainly Liverpool supporters, were crushed to death and some 170 injured on 15 April 1989. A similar situation had occurred on 4 February 1914, when a retaining wall collapsed injuring 75 people. As recently as 1981 South Yorkshire Police had told the owners of the ground that the crowd capacity was too high in the safety certificate for what proved to be the fatal end of the stadium.

Other relevant factors are design and the materials used, particularly where these have become outdated by a change in the pattern of use or superseded by products offering less risk. Crowd behaviour in confined spaces, even without large numbers, has to be taken into account. The general public is not trained to respond to an emergency and may quickly make a bad situation worse.

Individuals and small organisations are just as capable as large companies of doing widespread or serious damage. One abattoir or one person working in a shop or café can be a source of food poisoning. Someone driving a poorly maintained vehicle or going too fast in fog can cause a motorway pile-up. The possibilities for disasters are diverse.

Is there a common factor?

To some people they are all examples of a changed ethos, the shift from the values of public service to the vices of private profit, a focus on the short term at the expense of a wider vision. There are doubts about the division of responsibility with the privatisation of what was a unified rail network and the provision of gas by independent suppliers. The changed ethos may be a factor but is by no means the whole story.

To see what disasters have in common it is worth looking at two different ones in detail, the Aberfan tip slide in 1966 and the King's Cross Underground fire in 1987. The two events are separated by a generation, enabling us to see whether any significant lessons were learned.

Aberfan

Aberfan was a South Wales mining village, a tightly-knit community overshadowed by a mountain on which colliery waste had been tipped. On 21 October 1966 thousands of tons of this rubbish slid down into the village, killing 144 men, women and children. Of the victims, 116 were children.

The unanimous view of the public inquiry (Davies 1967) was unequivocal. Bracketed figures refer to sections of the Davies Report.
1. The Aberfan disaster could and should have been prevented. It was a matter not of wickedness but of ignorance, ineptitude and a failure in communication. Ignorance on the part of those charged at all levels with the siting, control and daily management of tips; bungling ineptitude on the part of those who had the duty of supervising and directing them; failure on the part of those having knowledge of the factors which affect tip safety to communicate that knowledge and to see that it was applied. (paragraph 18) There are no villains in this harrowing story: no villains, but decent men, led astray by foolishness or by ignorance or by both

in combination. (47) It is in the realm of an absence of policy that the gravest strictures lie, and it is that absence which must be the root cause of the disaster. (182)

2. The disaster was foreseeable. In 1927 Professor George Knox had delivered to the South Wales Institute of Engineers a paper 'Landslides in South Wales Valleys', which warned of the menace to tip stability through the uncontrolled presence of water. He predicted that if you do not pay for drainage you will have to pay for landslides in another way. (44) A 1939 memorandum on precautions to prevent sliding was amended and distributed in 1965, following an incident in the neighbouring National Coal Board (NCB) area, but received a limited distribution. (159–163) There were flow-slides at Aberfan in 1944 and 1963. The insouciance of the NCB following the substantial slide in 1963 was remarkable (135): the Board tried to maintain that there had been no slide. (154) In its pattern, the 1963 slide bore a striking resemblance to the fatal disaster. For nearly three years it presented a vivid warning of the terrible danger which loomed ahead. But it was a warning that no one in authority ever heeded. (145)

3. Previous slides had not taken a single human life. (42)

4. There were no statutory provisions on tip safety. (66/67/70)

5. Management structure and responsibilities did not match the situation. Although charged with responsibility for coal-tips, managers wholly lacked any special training to enable them to detect signs of instability. They were given no instructions as to how this should be done, they were not required to inspect, and apart from one solitary occasion in 1965 they had to render no report. Tip stability is a civil engineering problem, but no civil engineers were appointed even at the area level until 1958 and none was appointed at group level. Until they appeared at area level, all civil engineering matters were referred to the mechanical engineer. (65) There was a lack of collaboration between civil and mechanical engineers. (166)

6. Representations to the NCB by the local borough council as early as 1960 were given inadequate attention. (111) Further apprehensions were voiced at a colliery consultative committee after the 1963 slide. (136) After a councillor's outburst in the town

planning committee in 1964 there was a sorry tale of inertia and neglect, and one from which the taint of subterfuge and arrogance by the NCB was not wholly absent. The NCB gave empty assurances and the borough council accepted the opinions of NCB experts at face value. (146)

7. Not until two-thirds of the way through the official inquiry, and only then through cross-examination and not in frank admission, did the NCB accept responsibility for the disaster, initially trying to blame it on geology. (189–197) A statement by the NCB chairman to a television reporter two days after the disaster that it was impossible to know there was a spring at the heart of the tip was shown to be false. In his closing address counsel for the NCB invited the tribunal to ignore it. (198–206) The blame was shared among NCB headquarters, the division and the local management. Individual NCB officials were named as sharing the responsibility for the disaster.

The verdict of the inquest, adjourned until after the tribunal's findings, was accidental death.

King's Cross

The 31 deaths and other injuries in the King's Cross escalator and ticket hall fire on 18 November 1987 could have been prevented. The public inquiry identified several management shortcomings (Fennell 1988). Figures in brackets refer to sections of the report.

1. The risk was known. There had been 46 escalator fires between 1956 and 1988 and in two instances the cause was attributed to smokers' materials. (1.2) Between 1939 and 1944 there had been 77 fires on escalators of the King's Cross type, mainly attributed to the ignition by smokers' materials of accumulated dirt under escalators. On 24 December 1944 Bakerloo Line escalators at Paddington were completely gutted. (7.13) The report concluded that a disaster was foreseeable. (1.14)

2. The outbreak of fire was not regarded as something unusual; indeed it was regarded by senior management as inevitable with a system of this age. The attitude was no doubt increased by the insistence of London Transport management that fire should never be referred to as fire but by the euphemism 'smouldering'.

(10.4) They were lulled into a false sense of security by the fact that no previous escalator fire had caused a death. (1.15)

3. Management responsibility was not clear. London Regional Transport believed that all operational matters including safety were a matter for the operating company, London Underground. (1.11) No one person was charged with overall responsibility for safety. Each director believed he was responsible for safety in his division, but that it covered principally the safety of staff. The operations director, who was responsible for the safe operation of the system, did not believe he was responsible for the safety of lifts and escalators, which came within the engineering director's department. (1.17) There was no up-to-date or complete chart showing the level of responsibility at which decisions were being taken. (5.4)

4. London Underground had an inward-looking approach that undoubtedly led to a dangerous, blinkered self-sufficiency which included a general unwillingness to take advice or accept criticism from outside bodies. For example, advice from the London Fire Brigade regarding the importance and procedure for calling them went unheeded. (4.9)

5. London Underground had no evacuation plan (1.9) and no system to train staff in fire drill or evacuation. It failed to appreciate the particular problem of smoke. (1.18)

6. Supervision was sloppy. Staff on the late shift, in the habit of doubling or trebling their half-hour meal break, were not on duty when they should have been. (10.15/16)

7. Although smoking had been banned on the Underground in February 1985, following the fire at Oxford Circus station, the ban was not thoroughly enforced. (1.2)

At the inquest in October 1988, before the publication of the report in November, the coroner directed the jury to reach a verdict of accidental death.

The similarities between these two events are striking. They are certainly more remarkable than the differences.

Living in the ignorant present

We are not dealing with some novel phenomenon. Both disasters were foreseeable and preventable. The risks were not appreciated. Neither organisation learned from its own history, let alone anybody else's. Both operated in an ignorant present.

Incubation period
There was no single cause, no careless individual. The disasters were typified by what might be called an incubation period in which a number of events accumulated over time but went unnoticed or were misunderstood. Unlike a chapter of accidents, the process can be explained, unfortunately after the event. Moreover, as in understanding any major historical event, judgments can be made about the relative importance of various causes.

Re-defining reality
Instead of facing reality managers had redefined it to suit themselves. Previous incidents had not caused loss of life, leading managements to trust in providence rather than take preventive measures.

If we don't have to...
The absence of legislation was taken to mean that no problem existed.

Safety?
In what one would expect to be safety cultures the concept of safety was neither comprehensive nor universally comprehended.

Poor management
There were serious deficiencies in management organisation, definition of responsibilities and supervision.

Communication failures
There were failures in communication, ample evidence for the formula: energy + misinformation = disaster.

Errors and incorrect assumptions, either not perceived as such or regarded as unimportant at the time, gathered a collective weight and momentum of their own, driving inexorably towards a fatal conclusion. As so often, they were disasters waiting to happen.

Human failings
The failures were more personal than technical. The technology was more reliable than the use made of it.

Closed organisations

Outside help and criticism had been ignored. Both organisations had their own corporate culture, an institutional behaviour manifested in conditioned reflexes.

This comparison does not imply that history will repeat itself. It does not mean that we are destined at some time to experience a sequence of disasters on the scale of the latter half of the 1980s. Nobody can predict when and where the next disaster will occur.

What is certain is that prevention is better than cure. That means we all have to learn the lessons of history, not wait on legislation.

The price of safety is eternal vigilance. That demands a particular attitude of mind: not accepting bland assurances at face value, questioning, challenging, seeking all the time to improve in an ever-changing environment, engaging in creative thinking. Managements have to take the initiative in making it happen.

References

Davies Sir H. E. (1967) *Tribunal Appointed to Inquire into the Disaster at Aberfan on October 21st 1966 Report HL316 and HC 553* London: HMSO

Fennell, D. (1988) *Investigation into the King's Cross Underground Fire Cm 499* London: HMSO

2 ISSUES

Shirley Harrison

What are the responsibilities of managers in communicating at a time of disaster or crisis? This chapter raises some of the issues which managers could consider in preparing to deal with such events. The issues raised, while some may be used as guidelines in planning for a crisis or disaster response, are primarily intended to stimulate thinking and discussion in organisations and the news media which reports on them. Some practical ideas about training and rehearsal are given in Chapter 13.

Recognising stakeholders

An organisation's stakeholders can be thought of as all those individuals and groups of people who are involved in or affected by its activities, together with those who have the power to help or hinder it, for example by investing in it or regulating it. Some companies think of their stakeholders as those who have the most direct effect on their activities: shareholders, staff, suppliers, customers and the financial community. Others may cast the net wider to include their local community, pressure groups, the government and the media.

For the news media, stakeholder identification is also a useful exercise. Their most important stakeholders could be expected to be consumers, who will or will not be interested in buying the newspaper or tuning in to the news report. But, depending on the climate of opinion prevailing at the time, the government or the Press Complaints Commission or a single member of parliament, with a Private Member's Bill on statutory regulation of the press, may supersede in importance even the news-hungry public.

'The news media' is simply a convenient term for a wide range of news providers and there is no reason why one member of the media should list the same stakeholders, in the same order of priority, as any other. For example, the BBC, in its position as public broadcasting service, is likely to be more concerned with satisfying the needs of its stakeholders in the 'establishment'. A local newspaper, on the other hand, may have to balance its proprietor's requirement for a profit with its readers' local interests and concerns.

In considering the impact of a crisis or disaster on the organisation, recognising stakeholders is a crucial first stage. An organisation's managers might in any case want to agree on identifying its stakeholders and their relative power or influence over its successful existence. In doing so, they will be better able to plan for a response to their stakeholders before disaster strikes.

Employees

When managers undertake a stakeholder analysis they typically find that the staff of the organisation are crucial to its success. But when it comes to communicating in the heat of a disaster, employees are simply expected to pull together and get on with putting things right. Managers tend to give low priority, or even to forget, communication with their staff.

Why should good internal communication be vital in the normal run of events, yet disappear when the organisation has to deal with a crisis or emergency? The answer, clearly, is that it should not: the organisation under siege needs everyone who works for it to be operating at full stretch. They can only be expected to do this if they are working with good information. In the rush to organise a press briefing, this is easily forgotten. Staff who do not know what is going on nor what their employer's response is are not simply ill-informed and less able to do their job properly, though this can cause problems enough. In addition this can lead to resentment between those who are in the 'crisis team' – the celebrities who are getting special treatment and maybe even appearing on the telly – and those who are not. The latter consider themselves to be the 'carrying everything else team', seeing the situation as

We get an extra workload. They get extra resources.

They get extra recognition. We get even less recognition. (Casswell 1996)

Disasters have lasting effects on staff as well as on more readily identified victims and there is a view (Newburn 1996) that compulsory de-briefing should be seen as a crucial element in the care of staff.

Blame and responsibility

When a crisis or disaster happens, the natural questions are: whose fault was it and who is to blame? Although it may be convenient to have a scapegoat, the deeper question is: how did it happen – and how can we make sure it doesn't happen again? The nature of a crisis is that, once it breaks, events move fast. So the outcome of an investigation or inquiry will be too far after the event to answer the immediate question about responsibility. This is a question to which the media want answers right away. If no answer is forthcoming, speculation is likely to provide one. Those managers who, on reading the section above, did not immediately think of the media as a stakeholder may now want to reconsider.

There may be several strands to the issue of blame and responsibility. For example, following the Lockerbie air disaster, attention was not so much focused on who was responsible for the explosion on the plane – which terrorist group or individual – but more on how did the bomb get on the plane in the first place. Was the airline or airport security at fault? A perceived failure by the company to address this question posed by the media (on behalf, they would claim, of air travellers everywhere) is considered by analysts to have played a major part in the subsequent downfall of Pan Am.

A further example is provided by the Hillsborough disaster, dealt with in detail in Part III of this book. Within hours of the disaster reports began to circulate that the police had opened an exit gate at the football stadium, letting in 4,000 late arrivals. The Chief Constable was quoted as saying that the purpose of opening the gate was to save people's lives because of the crush outside. There was no shortage of eye witnesses and television footage to show what had happened, and what had caused the fatalities. But as with any disaster, the media were looking for new angles on the story from day one. In the case of Hillsborough, there was speculation about the role of the police, of ground officials, the behaviour of the fans, the design of the stadium – and all these were being mooted as possible contributory factors.

Thus the issues of blame and responsibility are crucial: to the media, to the general public, to the organisations concerned, who will be investigating internally to find out what went wrong, and of course, to the friends and relatives of the victims.

This issue is further complicated by the problem of compensation. Because the United Kingdom does not have a state 'no fault' compensation scheme, questions of blame and responsibility are bound up with the law and the need for someone to be sued, or found guilty of an offence, or proved negligent, before compensation can be paid to the victims.

This puts the organisation into a dilemma. On the one hand, the clamour from the media and the public is 'Who is to blame?' – and the organisation has to answer. On the other hand, lawyers – the organisation's own and its insurer's lawyers – will be insisting on 'No comment.' Coupled with this is the problem of the mismatch of time-scales mentioned above. The media and the public want answers now, but inquiries can take months or even years; and in the meantime the organisation has to do what it can for whoever is suffering from the effects of the crisis.

Hence the vital importance of good communication. In the first dilemma, a good press or public relations officer is expert in the careful handling of information and will have good contacts with and an understanding of the media. If anyone can tread the line between spilling too many beans, and no comment, such a person can. In the second problem, the organisation's communications professionals can get on with providing the answers and managing the flow of information while the operational side of the organisation gets on with putting things right.

This approach is also helpful from the media point of view. If there is someone responsible for providing all the necessary background information, for arranging interviews, press conferences and photo opportunities, a good deal of the mundane and time-consuming work is done. The reporter can concentrate on getting the story.

The management of reputation

Organisations which want to have a hand in how they are perceived, rather than simply let others comment on them, take the management of their reputation seriously. This takes many forms, from operating stringent quality control measures to putting staff through comprehensive induction and ongoing training in customer care. But as we saw in the introduction to Part I of this book, if a company is perceived to have dealt badly with a crisis or disaster then its reputation will be damaged, possibly irretrievably.

Elsewhere in this book there is ample advice on dealing with crises and disasters, from the media and from organisations that have been through the mill. The issue here is one of forward planning. Every organisation needs to have a strategy in place to address how it manages its reputation, and especially what it does to safeguard that reputation when disaster strikes.

Preparedness

Stakeholder identification gives managers a list of individuals and groups with whom communication is especially important. Scenario planning identifies not only what could happen but who might be involved in the response to a crisis or disaster. From this point it is relatively straightforward to produce a plan.

The planning process can be shown in the form of a model which builds up over eight stages, as shown in Figure 1. The stages are

- *direction:* making clear what the plan is designed to achieve, its aims and objectives
- *information gathering:* identifying stakeholders, scenario planning, considering resources needed, selecting a crisis management team, researching to learn from previous crises and disasters, advance preparation of background material
- *plan writing:* establishing management and team responsibilities, spokespeople, media arrangements, managing information flow and security
- *consultation:* wide discussion during and after the preparation of the plan with all those whose input would be helpful, including external organisations and individuals
- *publication:* the plan should be published in consultation with those concerned with it and it should be made available to all who will be involved in its execution

- *training:* the plan will throw up training requirements, which need to be met before it becomes operational
- *validation:* rehearsal in the form of exercises, real or 'table top', is the only way to ensure that the plan stands a chance of working in practice
- *confirmation or revision:* rehearsals and regular reviews are required in order to keep the plan up-to-date and workable.

Figure 1 The planning cycle
Source: Emergency Planning College

A number of questions arise from this process. For example, how public is the plan to be made, during its production and subsequently? If the plan is entirely in the public domain, that may constrain its authors or lead to the publication of a plan for public consumption which is different from the 'real' plan. Another question is how to include representatives of the media. Journalists could be involved in putting the plan together, or be brought in at the validation stage to play their part in rehearsals. Some companies use journalists to deliver training in media handling to their managers.

It is convenient to list the eight stages in this way. But planning for the response to a crisis or disaster is not a question of following a list of procedures. The very process of producing a written plan, guide or manual can take responsibility and ownership away from most people in the organisation. Staff may think that, if their name does not appear as a major player in the plan, then they are not involved and they bear no responsibility. Similarly, a lengthy written document which seeks to cover every eventuality may be ignored because it is too detailed – no-one can possibly remember everything in it. It can also lead to complacency on the grounds that if it isn't in the plan, it won't happen.

Even the best prepared plan will not be able to cover all eventualities. All disasters are different in some way or another. But

> If the worst happens, it will call for qualities of leadership, decisiveness, speed, creativity and flexibility as well as skills … such as sound organisation, order, method and technical ability. (Bradford 1986)

What-if scenario planning

Crises and disasters tend by their very nature to hit organisations hard, but the immediate instinct to panic can be subdued if the element of surprise is mitigated by scenario planning. What if a terrorist attack wrecked the company's flagship store? What if the management team was away on a team-building exercise and their boat capsized? What if there was a fire at headquarters? What if the computer system was invaded by a bug which corrupted all its records? What if the company's best-selling product was tampered with and caused accidents? How many skeletons has the organisation got lurking in its cupboards, and what if they got out? Organisations which are involved with potentially hazardous or harmful undertakings, such as transport, the nuclear industry and petrochemicals are well used to scenario planning. Local authorities, hospitals, the utilities and the emergency services generally undertake it as a matter of course. But it is not so common elsewhere.

It makes sense for scenario planning to include a wide range of staff from all parts of the organisation. They can get together in brainstorming sessions, preferably with an outside facilitator, and think through all the possible disasters with which their organisation could be involved. It is then easier to consider how plans should be made first, for avoiding them, and then, for responding to them.

Communication planning

A plan for responding to a crisis or disaster needs to make clear how lines of communication will work. Who is to speak on what issue and what can they say? How will they get their message across and to whom? How will information flow be managed into, within and out of the organisation?

The news media will immediately deploy their reporters, film crews, photographers and radio cars. The organisation to which they may very well lay siege needs to be prepared.

A communication plan for crises and disasters will take account of who is to speak for the organisation. The media's preference is for the most senior person and indeed it can look distinctly odd if the chief executive officer is not available for comment – what are you trying to hide? But it may be that the person who is most expert on the subject, or the best performer in a television studio is the best person to speak. Certainly there is an issue here about forward planning. Whoever is going to face the press, the microphones and the cameras needs to be fully equipped to do so, which may have training implications for the organisation.

The issue of co-ordination needs to be addressed. If there is to be more than one spokesperson, how will co-ordination be achieved? A form of internal briefing might be necessary. In any case, it is advisable to have some method of disseminating information to the staff in the organisation, so that they know what is going on, what is being said, and what the organisation is doing.

What can you say?

This will always depend on circumstances, but one thing which is fairly certain is that the communications professional will always want to say more than the organisation's lawyer will want them to. From the point of view of good relations with stakeholders, however, it makes sense to express sorrow or regret. Saying you are sorry does not need to imply that it was your fault. It is a perfectly proper human response to a tragedy. Beyond expressions of regret and sympathy, it is wise simply to stick to the facts. Providing information is the best way to damp down speculation.

It is also good advice to own up where mistakes have been made. From the point of view of the organisation's reputation, being found out in some kind of cover-up is the kiss of death. However, if there are inquiries and legal proceedings, it can be difficult for an organisation to know how to comment without prejudicing the outcome. An example of the right way of doing it comes from another football disaster, that of the fire in the old wooden stand at Bradford City's football stadium in 1985, at which 56 people died.

West Yorkshire Metropolitan District Council, as it then was, had written to Bradford City Football Club a few months before the fire, with a warning about the stand '... the timber construction is a fire hazard...' the letter said '... a carelessly discarded cigarette could give rise to a fire risk...'. The club was then in the third division, but by the time of the disaster they were due to be promoted to the second, when they would require a general safety certificate. West Yorkshire and Bradford councils, the police and the fire service had planned a meeting to discuss the safety certificate for the Wednesday following the match. The stand itself was due for demolition two days after the match. Copies of the letters warning of fire risk had been sent to Bradford council at the same time as the football club had received theirs. The implication was that the warnings had been ignored. Three days after the disaster, the chief executive of Bradford council issued a press statement acknowledging that the letters had been received and explaining why the council had been powerless to act – because responsibility for ground safety was not yet theirs. A press officer said later

> It was very much the right thing to do. We owned up right away, as soon as we knew we had done something which could be seriously criticised. (Bradford 1986)

In fact, the statement was duly printed in the local press without further comment, and that was the end of that particular angle on the story. Imagine how differently the story would have been treated if a reporter had found out about the warning letters from some other source. Even if the council had been given the opportunity to comment, the chief executive would have been put on the defensive, having to justify the council's apparent inaction.

In the final part of this chapter let us leave aside the skills and the practicalities and look more closely at one of the qualities needed.

Telling the truth

When all the consultation and planning has been done, however methodical, the organisation hit by crisis or disaster has to act on the day in the light of the circumstances that arise. In such a situation the organisation needs to have a firm platform from which to deliver its message. While the crisis management plan can provide this to an extent, in the form of check lists and guidelines, the communications professional may do better to consider, simply, how to behave.

Research conducted in the period 1994–6 at the Emergency Planning College (Harrison 1997) asked those whose job is to give or obtain information about a crisis or disaster whether they had any kind of guidance as to how to behave. Some could, and did, refer to codes of conduct or guidelines on good practice; others were guided by operational instructions or special procedures which were laid down for emergencies. Many, however, simply relied on their own, informal guidelines: be truthful, be helpful, be honest, only give the facts. Others were more circumspect: speak carefully, don't trust the press, check for political consequences. Other comments reflected a more pragmatic view: it depends on circumstances, you need an in-built news sense. When it came to questions about telling the truth, it was found that practitioners have to use their own judgment and moral sense to distinguish between truths, half-truths and lies.

Telling the truth about a disaster, crisis or emergency may require a degree of courage on the part of the organisation. But as we saw earlier in the Bradford example, it is infinitely better to have told the truth than to have been found out hiding something questionable. Managers need have no fear of the media, even at a time of crisis or disaster, as long as they act with integrity. The chief executive of the West Wales Ambulance Trust is content for its employees to say what they like, when they like to the media because

> if anything was wrong we would already be dealing with it
> … If trust managers are afraid of exposure, it must mean
> that they are not confident in their own ability.
> (Fursland 1996)

Clearly the 'good' of telling the truth may sometimes have to be balanced against some other 'good' such as preserving patient confidentiality or being hurtful and insensitive. But when being open and honest has to be balanced against the 'good' of commercial considerations, companies might find the contest less equal. Here is another issue which managements would do well to debate.

Reporting the truth

The job of those in the news media is to report on events. Most of the time, the facts are not an issue. Newspaper editors may differ in their judgment as to which story is the most important, though television news reports tend to lead with the same item. Different publications take differing lines according to their political affiliations, proprietors' interests or readers' concerns. On the whole, however, the various elements of the media report the news as accurately as they are able within the constraints under which they work.

In Parts II and III of this book the chapters written by television, radio and newspaper journalists give compelling descriptions of the process of news gathering. Sometimes that process is made very difficult because reporters are shut out from events or information. When they cannot get the full story, they sometimes run with whatever they can get. In such cases the resulting coverage may be partial in both senses of the word.

Reporters are supposed to be impartial. They are not supposed to get personally involved in events, and certainly not to alter the course of events by any involvement they may inadvertently have. They are not supposed to take sides, although the company they work for might. They are traditionally supposed to report what happens in a dispassionate and objective way. However, in recent times the lines separating fact from opinion have become increasingly difficult to draw. Feature articles and essays take the facts and present them from a subjective point of view. Opinions differ on whether this matters, or whether the reader, viewer or listener should be trusted to make their own mind up about the accuracy of what they read and hear.

However, the principle of 'bystander journalism' is being increasingly questioned. Shortly before he left his job as the BBC's senior war correspondent to stand for election as an independent candidate in the May 1997 general election, Martin Bell made the case for what he called 'the journalism of attachment'.

By this I mean a journalism that cares as well as knows; that is aware of its responsibilities; and will not stand neutrally between good and evil, right and wrong, victim and oppressor. We in the press, and especially in television, do not stand apart from the world. We are a part of it. We exercise a certain influence, and we have to know that. The influence may be for better or for worse, and we have to know that too. (Bell 1997)

He cites as an example a story about a reporter in Sarajevo preparing a profile on a sniper. At the front line, the reporter, having asked the sniper what he could see, was told 'I see two people walking down the street – which of them do you want me to shoot?' As the reporter turned to leave, realising he had made a big mistake, the sound of gunfire rang out behind him and the sniper said 'That was a pity. You could have saved one of their lives.'

While Bell's view of the reporter as one who can change the course of events is doubtless the exception, we are seeing more examples of reporters' impartiality being affected by the events they cover. The Dunblane tragedy, discussed briefly in Chapter 15, is perhaps the clearest example of journalists becoming emotionally involved. The behaviour of journalists at Dunblane, in contrast to Hillsborough, indicates a change in attitude which may prove to be lasting, according to Nick Buckley of the *Mail on Sunday*

It was a valuable lesson for all concerned; that we, the journalists, the community and the police, can find a way of dealing with it. (IPI 1996)

In Part II we will see how journalists, communities, the police, civil servants, company spokespeople and others found ways of dealing with the crises, disasters and emergencies with which they were confronted.

References

Bell, M. (1997) 'Here is the war, live by satellite' London: *Guardian* 8 March. See also *British Journalism Review* March 1997

Bradford Council (1986) *Out of the Valley: Bradford MDC's response to the Bradford City Fire Disaster 1985–1986* Bradford: Policy Unit

Casswell, T. (1996) 'The Hillsborough Report: a summary in pictures' in *Journeys of Discovery: creative learning from disaster* London: National Institute for Social Work

Fursland, E. (1996) 'Still Gagging on the Truth' London: *Guardian* 20 July

Harrison, S. (1997) 'Earning trust by telling the truth: how should public relations and media professionals behave when a disaster happens?' *Journal of Communication Management* Volume 1 Number 3, February

IPI (1996) *Dunblane: reflecting tragedy* London: British Executive of the International Press Institute

Newburn, T. (1996) 'Some Lessons from Hillsborough' in *Journeys of Discovery: creative learning from disaster* London: National Institute for Social Work

PART II

CRISIS, EMERGENCY AND DISASTER

CRISIS, EMERGENCY AND DISASTER

The six chapters which follow this introduction will take you from rural Scotland to the hills of northern Iraq, from the river Thames to the North Sea, from a bombing in Oklahoma to a factory fire in Bradford. You will be taken there by an expert guide, for each chapter is written by someone who worked on the crisis, emergency or disaster which is described.

The chapters can be loosely divided into those written from the perspective of the media who were trying to report the disaster, and those relating the experience of the press or public relations manager on the scene. They explain how a variety of crises and disasters were managed by the organisations concerned and reported by the media. The purpose of this, the major part of the book, is to put the reader as nearly as possible into the shoes of the communication professionals who were on the ground on the day.

Each contributor speaks from personal experience about the events with which they have been involved, and which were, for them and for others caught up in them, probably of all-consuming interest at that time. But it is important not to dismiss these incidents as simply isolated events.

For example, John Jefferson describes in Chapter 5 how reports came in to BBC local radio of a commuter plane which crashed into a Yorkshire barley field on 24 May 1995. Fortunately this kind of incident does not happen every day. But in the not untypical week which followed, there were disasters of various kinds all over the world, as Table 2 shows.

Some of these disasters made news in Britain but most did not. We begin, in this part of the book, to get some clues as to why that might be. The differences between what constitutes a local, national or global news story are sharply drawn out in Clive Ferguson's chapter, which opens Part II. He explains how the BBC wants to be first with the news. Television news needs pictures, preferably action shots in which something is happening. If news-gatherers are not given access to shoot those pictures they will still try and get them somehow.

Date	Incident
24 May	UK, North Yorkshire: commuter plane crashes; 12 dead
25 May	Malacca: bulk tankers collide, fire ensues
26 May	South China Seas: oil tanker and container ship collide
26 May	Japan: two freighters collide; 3 crew members lost
27 May	Spain: freighter carrying wood pulp catches fire
27 May	Aden: fire at arms dump; sends missiles into people's houses
28 May	Russia: earthquake hits Sakhalin; over 2000 dead, 230 oil wells damaged and extensive pollution
29 May	Portugal: vapours from cargo of coal kills surveyors
29 May	China: flooding leaves 110,000 people homeless
30 May	USA: tornado kills 3, injures 20
30 May	Zaire: death toll from Ebola virus reaches 153
30 May	Japan: hydrogen sulphide leak at oil refinery injures 5
31 May	USA: air force jet crashes into flats; 3 dead, 2 missing
31 May	Brazil: mud slides kill 41, 45 others missing
31 May	Albania: hailstorms and heavy rain cause deaths of 2 children

Table 2 Disasters 24–31 May 1995
Source: Emergency Planning College

Chapter 4 gives an idea of how officialdom is involved at a time of national crisis or disaster, how Regional Emergency Committees work, which VIPs are likely to want to visit the scene and how the Central Office of Information can be drafted in to help with the media onslaught.

The component parts of the local news scene are described in Chapter 5, and there are useful explanations about the likely format for different types of interview, together with suggestions about preparation and training for those likely to have to act as spokespeople for their organisations. With the help of a carefully constructed timetable of events, we see how the Knight Air crash got on to the local and national news agenda that evening.

In Chapter 6 we see how a local radio station works, and how it can be an ally in a crisis. Local newspapers, radio and television often see themselves as the voice of their local community and at a time of crisis or disaster they are particularly concerned to ask the questions which their readers or listeners want answered. Using the graphic example of a major fire at a factory in Bradford, John Jefferson shows how this opportunity to speak directly to local people was missed by most of the protagonists.

Chapter 7 takes us from the local to the global scene, and recounts some of the problems of communicating in a major international emergency, that of Operation Safe Haven in northern Iraq. Tom Hardie-Forsyth deals with communication in the broadest sense, not simply confining himself to dealing with the media. He writes a very personal account in which his views about how good communication could have improved matters for the local communities are made absolutely clear, and he contends that the role of the media in this can be for the good – or the reverse.

The issues and practicalities of handling the media at a time of crisis or disaster are covered in Chapter 8, together with some proven strategies. Using a number of examples, Mike Granatt shows how the media process can be divided into four recognisable phases: mayhem, mastermind, manhunt and epilogue, and he provides a helpful check list as a starting point for each one.

Whether you are a press officer, a newspaper reporter, a police officer, a media manager, a hospital administrator, a lawyer, a charity worker, a company director, a safety expert, an emergency planner, a student or simply an interested member of the public, it is hoped that this part of the book you will strike a chord with you.

3 TELEVISION NEWS

Clive Ferguson

If you are the person responsible for dealing with the media, perhaps the most important thing you will have to come to terms with very quickly when you are dealing with a major, or even in some cases, a minor emergency is the numbers. You will be inundated with phone calls. I think it's fair to say that until you've been at the centre or even on the fringes of a King's Cross, a Piper Alpha, or something as tragically sad as Dunblane, you simply just can't imagine what it's going to be like. You may have had rehearsals and run exercises, you may have read the Home Office guidelines. Believe me, they do not exaggerate about the numbers of people you will have to deal with.

You will have local papers, local news agencies, local radio (BBC and independent local radio), local television – BBC and ITV – and probably from more than one region, national papers, national news agencies, national radio, national television, and in some cases, the international media, too: more radio, television, news agencies and newspapers.

To give you some idea, from my point of view, there is a rule of thumb for deployments of camera crews and so on at the first hint or report of a major incident: think of the number you think you need to cover the story properly – and then double it. That means not just people, but also 'hardware': mobile satellite vehicles, mobile editing, radio cars, radio production facilities, as well as producers, presenters, correspondents, camera crews and so on. Why? Because I win no prizes if I don't have enough people on the ground, close to the scene, in order to provide coverage across radio and television. To cover the story properly, I need to ensure that the BBC is at all the right places: news conferences, photo opportunities, on all the right doorsteps, gathering the material – be it sound or vision or both – to enable the BBC to tell the story in the fullest and most comprehensive manner.

You will also need to bear in mind that these days, there really is no such thing as the next deadline. The BBC already has a 24 hours a day radio news channel in the shape of Radio Five Live – and has recently launched a 24 hours a day television news channel. Sky News is already on the air. Even without a 24-hour facility, we in the BBC could and frequently did go 'live' on BBC 1 and BBC 2 whenever a major story broke – and we did that much more often than our main competitor, ITN.

That means that we will be using every means at our disposal to get to the scene – or as close as we are allowed to get – as soon as possible after the first hint of any incident. And while our camera crews and correspondents are en route we will be on the phone, perhaps talking to a spokesperson 'live' on radio or television, to let our viewers and listeners know what he or she knows about what's happened, or in some cases what may be still happening.

We are in the business of getting information as quickly as possible and then relaying that information as rapidly as possible to our audience. What we are *not* in the business of is putting out incorrect information. We want to be both first and right every time, but we will go out of our way to ensure that we are never first and wrong.

The person on the end of that phone – the company spokesperson, press officer or whoever – needs to know that they can say 'I'm sorry, I don't know the answer to that'. The BBC does not wish to speculate. Facts are what we deal in and what we want. We are mindful that people don't always have all the facts at their fingertips when we wish them to have.

It is worth remembering, however that we can be a very useful tool for the organisation to use. How else could you get the message across to so many people to avoid an area? If you believe the public could be in danger, for example, what better way than to use our means of mass communication to help you do just that? We want to help disseminate accurate facts: it's not simply our lust for news, we can play a vital role in allaying the fears of people around the country. Imagine how important it would be for you to know that that plane which crashed in Amsterdam was a cargo flight to Algeria, and not the British Midland flight to Schiphol from Heathrow, on which some members of your family were flying to Holland for a long weekend.

That's why we have what may seem to be an obsession with such minute details as flight numbers, train times and so on.

We are mindful that reporting of disasters – and they don't always have to be major ones – can cause alarm and distress. We are as anxious as you are to keep that distress to a minimum. There have been many examples of 'how not to do it'.

During the Falklands War, the Ministry of Defence announced the loss of a ship in the south Atlantic – and then didn't tell anyone which one. I'm sure you can imagine being the relative of one of the many servicemen on ships in the south Atlantic and hearing that sort of announcement. How many people were worried unnecessarily? What would have been going through your mind, do you think, as you watched or listened to that announcement? I don't think the M.o.D. would make the same type of announcement today. Indeed, I am sure that very few people would make the same mistake again.

Concern for next of kin of those reportedly killed or injured calls for special care. The BBC has adopted a strong general rule that, as far as is reasonably possible, next of kin should not learn this bad news from a radio or television programme. We recognise, however, that when names are not given, the news may cause needless concern among people with close relatives who might have been involved. In the choice between difficult options, we believe that this is not as bad as the shock caused when names are received, for the first time, by radio or television.

However, as the BBC's *Producers' Guidelines* point out,

> we also need to reduce needless anxiety by narrowing the area of concern as quickly as we can without identifying individual victims. (BBC 1993)

Hence our wish to include such details as airline name, flight number, place of departure, destination, so as to avoid alarming even larger numbers of people.

That is one reason why we need to have good quality information given to us – and why it's vitally important that the person who is acting as spokesperson must have as up to date knowledge as possible, and have the authority to impart that information to us.

One of the best examples of good practice was the interview given by Michael Bishop, the then chief executive of British Midland, at the scene of the plane crash at Kegworth some years ago. He provided factual replies to questions, did not speculate, and gave clear and concise answers. Equally we have seen how people can get it wrong, by being tempted to 'busk it' at news conferences. The police at the Hillsborough tragedy initially gave us to understand that their opening of the gates had absolutely no connection with the tragic events inside the stadium – something we now know to be patently untrue.

The most important thing I would stress is 'be honest'. Don't try to make it up as you go along. If you don't know then say so. Equally, if you do know, then give the answers, otherwise you appear to be hiding something. Maybe not there and then, but at some later point, you will be found out. It is worth remembering that the hacks you are dealing with will almost certainly have been involved in more of these incidents that you have – and their instincts will tell them if you are being 'economical with the truth'. Be up front, because if you're not, believe me, you will be found out, and then you will have a much worse public relations problem to handle than if you had been open and honest in the first place.

You need to help us to help you. The person giving us the information, either in the first few minutes on the phone, or later at the scene, has got to be credible, and has got to know what he or she is talking about. They must have the most up to date information. That relationship between your spokesperson and the media is of vital importance – to you and to us. It can make things run well, or it can make things start off so badly, that you never get a chance to recover.

As I mentioned earlier, you will get a lot of phone calls from the BBC, from Sky, from ITN, from the papers and so on. We at least do try to cut down those calls. We set up our own 'incident desk', so that instead of every single television programme calling you, we hope to cut those numbers right down. We know that the last thing you need is to have put the phone down having finished talking to one person from the BBC's television news room, simply to pick it up and have to speak to yet another person from another BBC television news programme. We know you, too, have a job to do, and while we can't guarantee to succeed in limiting those calls all the time, we do try.

It's worth pointing out that your media desk, or incident desk is a vitally important part of the whole operation, for you and for us. Townsend Thoresen didn't realise that in the initial period after the

Herald of Free Enterprise incident – they used the same phone lines for relatives' inquiries *and* for media inquiries. You can, I am sure, imagine the result. The whole system collapsed in a matter of a few hours, and many of the relatives of those aboard the ship got their information from us, from radio and television.

So, where should that main media centre be – at the headquarters or at the scene? The short answer is it may need to be at both.

Now we all hope, honestly we do, that we never have to cover something as dreadful as the events in Dunblane. But we do have a job to do – to report, to investigate, to analyse. I must say that our correspondents and producers who reported from Dunblane were full of praise for how well things were organised on the ground. A hall was set up as the media centre. Phones were provided for every news organisation. Power points were provided for computers and the rest of the paraphernalia with which we now travel everywhere. News conferences were held regularly, as were briefings from those in charge. Requests were dealt with fairly – and they rapidly provided access to, for example, to the Scottish Secretary of State, and his shadow.

As I said earlier, we all hope never to have to be involved in such a disaster, from whichever side of the fence we are on. But this was a huge story for us. Can you imagine the numbers at Dunblane? Estimates ranged from 400 to 600 journalists and technicians in Dunblane, a city of some 7000 residents. There was, undoubtedly a real risk that the citizens of Dunblane, and not just those who were directly involved in the tragedy, but the other residents, too, would simply be swamped by such a large media presence.

But Dunblane provides us with, I think, the best example of how we can be trusted. In spite of the numbers, and in spite of all the rumours, I think that if you talk to the police and the emergency services who were involved, they will confirm that we respected people's feelings. And that respect for people's feelings is surely best demonstrated by the BBC's decision to lead the pack and not send journalists or cameras to the children's funerals. And indeed, we also took the decision to return to the school only when invited to do so by the head teacher.

I believe that demonstrated that we can, do and will act responsibly and with sensitivity.

We worked with the local emergency services throughout, which proved to be to everyone's benefit, I feel.

I think it's also important to point out that our decision not to be at the funerals was not decided from a distance and on high in London. We in London were, in fact, responding to guidance from our producer on the ground in Dunblane, who was relaying to us what relatives and families were telling the police. It was her advice which influenced our decision. That I believe shows that the people we employ are sensitive to such issues, they are aware of what is expected of them by the BBC, but also what is expected of them by the public. They may not have memorised the nearly three hundred pages of the *Producers' Guidelines*, but they know of the content and of how important are those guidelines to the BBC's reputation.

The *Producers' Guidelines* codify the good practice which has been established through the dedication to public service broadcasting of generations of programme makers. Today, as the Director General says in his foreword to the latest edition of those guidelines, we expect producers and editors to value that good practice as our audiences clearly do.

I like to think that the example of what happened over our coverage of the aftermath of Dunblane reassures people that our journalists display the correct degree of sensitivity. But I think it is also worth pointing out that the staff in the BBC work to 'guidelines'. These are not rules that can never be broken. They are there to guide our staff – and to reassure the public, our audience, of our commitment to our high editorial standards. They are there to guide producers, editors, correspondents to reach the correct decision. But, of course, a different decision may be taken should, heaven forbid, we ever be faced with such circumstances again, as we were in Dunblane.

Those same guidelines also make reference to 'revisiting' tragic events, by way of re-using pictures, known to us as 'library pictures', some time after the original event. They warn against the 'needless repetition of traumatic library material, especially if it features identifiable people'. We already insist that our journalists re-use only certain images from, for example, our coverage at the time of Piper Alpha, and Hillsborough.

Access to the scene of any disaster is perhaps the thorniest of subjects – second only, I suppose, to the interviewing of victims, or relatives of victims. We do want to get as close as possible to the scene of an incident, not because we are ghouls, but because we need to record the sound and the pictures to enable us to tell the story. We do not want to get in your way, and indeed our own guidelines on safety mean we do not want get ourselves killed or injured.

But we do want to talk to people who wish to talk to us, either 'live' or pre-recorded. At the scene of the bombing in Oklahoma, for example, the emergency services channelled requests through to not just their own staff – such as chief police officers, and fire officers – but also to members of the public who had themselves been caught up in the event. They also laid on a 'press pen', not miles from the scene, but close to where things were happening, allowing us to get the pictures and the sound we needed, but stopping the media from intruding either on private grief, or on areas which could still have contained vital clues or evidence which could lead to the arrest of the perpetrators of the bombing.

And, of course, we do not need to be in the middle of such scenes – we could be standing in front of a fire appliance, or police car – we merely need to be somewhere we can be seen to be close to the action.

It's worth remembering that we are easy to control. You can make use of the pooling system. That is when one broadcaster will take the pictures or do the interviews but then make them available to everyone. Now we will not always want to pool the gathering of interviews or pictures, but we will go along with the request if there is a very good reason, and that reason is explained to us. Dunblane threw up several examples of pooling. Clearly we would not and did not wish to have hordes of camera crews and correspondents crawling over everyone in the city. It was a BBC camera which was selected to get close-up pictures of the exterior of the school. No-one wished to have pictures of the inside of the gym. I feel that no-one would have wished to have recorded such pictures even if they had been offered. At the hospital, too, news conferences with the parents of the injured lessened the number of times people had to give interviews.

Now, the advantages to you are clear. You control access to the scene or site, and you don't have great hordes of people trampling over evidence. From our point of view, we know that no-one is getting anything to which we are denied access. Indeed, from the

BBC's point of view, I believe we may have fewer problems with pooling than our competitors, for the simple reason that whatever the pictures, we believe that we employ the better journalists. So even if we all get exactly the same material, at the end of the day, we think our product will be better.

A word of warning, though: if you do decide to organise a pool, do not try to set it up yourself. Leave it to the broadcasters to sort out. We do it all the time, and it means that we will only have ourselves to blame if it all goes wrong – and you can emerge untarnished, and still be friends with everyone.

Of course, you can choose not to work with us, to ignore all this advice, and simply keep us all far away from the scene, and not give us any access or information. Or you could try.

Don't forget that for almost any one of us at the scene of an emergency, it will not be our first. We will know all the ways of getting around whatever barriers you put in our way. Now you might find that one or two will play ball and stand quietly behind the blue and white tape for hours on end while no-one is telling them anything, but I doubt it. It will not take very long, often only minutes after you've rebuffed a request, before the camera crews and the correspondents are off across the fields, or down a back alley-way, or up on to a roof. But, work with us and I believe we will not reinforce your worst impressions of us.

Of course, the other reason people try to keep the cameras away from the scene is for reasons they justify on the grounds of taste. To them I would say: leave such judgements to the professionals. Day in, day out we are making decisions on the grounds of taste. We know what we are doing. We know, through our research, what the public want to see and what they do not want to see. We know how to treat such scenes so as not to alienate our audience, and also, if not more importantly, not to offend. You will all have heard on our programmes the following expression 'you may find some of the pictures in this report disturbing', or words to that effect.

The BBC already has a well established policy of making nine o'clock in the evening the pivotal point of the evening's television, a watershed before which, except in exceptional circumstance, all programmes on our domestic channels should be suitable for a general audience, including children. The earlier in the evening a programme is placed, the more suitable it is likely to be for children to watch on their own, though the BBC expects parents, too, to share the responsibility for assessing whether or not individual programmes should be seen by younger viewers.

The BBC has made, for its internal training purposes, a video entitled *Violence in the News*, which is shown to camera crews, producers, correspondents, and editors – indeed to anyone who may have to make editorial decisions on ground of taste and decency. It demonstrates – often in graphic detail – what our own guidelines have led us to leave out of out television news reports.

It is a balancing act. There is a balance to be struck between the demands of truth and the danger of desensitising people. With some news stories a sense of shock is part of a full understanding of what has happened. However, the more often we shock our viewers, the more it will take to shock them.

The video re-iterates points made in our *Producers' Guidelines*

- the dead should be treated with respect and not shown unless there are compelling reasons to do so

- close-ups should generally be avoided

- do not concentrate unduly on the bloody consequences of an accident or terrorist attack

- avoid using violent material simply because it is available.

- the same value should be placed on human life and suffering whether it occurs at home or overseas

To that end, we frequently leave on the cutting room floor the bloodiest of footage that either our camera crews have recorded, or which is being offered to us by picture agencies. But we believe that doesn't necessarily result in a sanitised version of events. A good script, we believe, is vital in conveying the reality of tragedy.

As I have mentioned before, we all genuinely hope not have to be present, or to cover tragic events. Sadly human nature and indeed nature itself seems likely to mean that hope will not be realised. However, I know that my correspondents and producers and camera crews will remember all this the next time they are at the scene of a disaster. I know because they will be reminded, as indeed they were when they covered the events in Dunblane. I trust that you, too, will appreciate what they are doing, how and why they are doing it – and that you will work with them, not against, when next your paths cross.

Reference

BBC (1993) *Producers' Guidelines* London: British Broadcasting
Corporation

4 THE NATIONAL CRISIS

Peter Whitbread

In common with other post-industrial societies, Britain has a complex infrastructure of transport, utilities, industry, food and social networks. Under normal circumstances we go about our business without giving these essentials a thought, but when they break down the situation can quickly escalate to crisis proportions. Fortunately, although increasing, such breakdown is still rare; despite the complexity of our society few of us will ever be directly affected. Moreover, where such breakdown has occurred in recent years, the crisis has been contained at a local or regional level.

The risk of war is probably lower than it has ever been, and the United Kingdom is enjoying more cordial industrial relations, better health care and improving safety and environmental management. Nevertheless, a national crisis could strike at any time.

There has been considerable debate about the terms used to describe hazard and disaster. Some definition issues are discussed by Parker and Handmer (1992). However, for the purposes of this chapter, situations which could be defined as a national crisis include events like those shown in the following paragraphs.

A national crisis can include 'natural' disasters such as large scale flooding, hurricanes or health epidemics, 'man-made' disasters such as terrorist bomb attacks, wars or national strikes in essential services, and accidents such as the Chernobyl nuclear reactor explosion.

A national crisis could also develop as the result of a chronic problem suddenly turning into an acute incident. Situations such as the possibility of regional water shortages being exacerbated by a national drought, or discovery of major weaknesses in the food chain could come into this category. In recent years much media attention has been paid to the unpredictable and potentially devastating effects of BSE in Britain, the Ebola virus in Africa, and the spread of HIV. Although the 'worst case' scenarios posited by the media and pundits have so far not materialised, no official would be sufficiently brave or foolhardy to suggest that protective measures and contingency plans should be dismantled.

Routine emergencies	Disasters
Interaction with familiar faces	Interaction with unfamiliar faces
Familiar tasks and procedures	Unfamiliar tasks and procedures
Intra-organisational co-ordination needed	Intra- and inter-organisational co-ordination needed
Roads, telephones, facilities intact	Roads blocked or jammed, telephones jammed or non-functional, facilities damaged
Communications frequencies adequate for radio traffic	Radio frequencies often overloaded
Communication intra-organisational	Need for inter-organisational information sharing
Use of familiar terminology in communicating	Communication with persons who use different terminology or speak another language
Need to deal mainly with local press	Hordes of national and international reporters
Management structure adequate to co-ordinate the number of resources involved	Resources often exceed management capacity

Table 3 Differences between routine emergencies and disasters
Source: Auf der Heide 1989

For planning purposes, it is useful to use a geographical measure to define the scale of the crisis. Many crises will come under the regional umbrella; examples of a local or regional crisis include such disasters as the Hillsborough Stadium deaths, and terrorist bombs such as the Manchester bombing in 1996. Where the IRA bomb explosion in Manchester might be considered as a local emergency, the terrorist bomb over Lockerbie on Pan Am flight 103 from Frankfurt to New York was an international incident. The essential difference between the two was that the bomb had been loaded onto an American plane which commenced its journey in Germany, contained passengers from many different countries, and which exploded over Britain.

Whether local, regional, national or international, what all acute catastrophes have in common is their unpredictability, the speed at which they strike and often the need for emergency services to mobilise and deliver exceptional help in circumstances where even ordinary activities are incredibly hampered.

What these crises also have in common is the increasingly efficient and effective way they are handled by the emergency services, who have used the lessons learned from the past to refine and improve their performance.

There are a number of different terms used to describe a crisis, such as accident, disaster, emergency, and it may be useful to consider the essential differences between a 'routine' emergency, and a disaster. Table 3 sets out some distinguishing characteristics.

One of the most marked characteristics of a crisis is the unexpected escalation of events, and it is this very unexpectedness which appears to make it difficult to plan. However there are common factors, and a detailed plan of action gives the best possible chance to deal quickly and effectively with whatever situation arises.

Berge (1988) lists the external factors which tend to be common to crisis situations as damage; an escalating flow of events; that time is not on your side; the media will descend in large numbers; and that rumour and speculation will tend to run wild.

A national crisis could be an ongoing situation, with the potential for further and increasing damage, such as a health epidemic, or it could be a one-off, such as a terrorist attack. In the former, plans will include measures to manage and contain the devastation; in the latter type of crisis the main tasks are to assess the damage, and deal with survivors, victims and their families. In both types of situation the task of communication is a vital and integral part of the job. Indeed, in the case of a crisis which has passed it is probably the major task, and regardless of how well it is dealt with, the overriding impression which the public will take away will be informed by how well the crisis has been communicated. It can take years to correct damaging impressions. Sometimes they can never be corrected at all.

In the UK, emergency planning comes under the remit of the Home Office Emergency Planning Division.

'Integrated Emergency Management' is the term which is used to describe the management of the process by which action is taken to protect life, property, the community and the environment, and to reduce the vulnerability of individuals and the community to disasters. Its basic principles are risk assessment, accident prevention, emergency planning and incident response and recovery.

The basic principle underlying the national approach to the handling of a crisis, whatever its size or scope, is that the first response to an emergency will be at the place where the emergency occurs, that is, at the local level. The response is likely to involve the emergency services and local authority. It can also of course include many other organisations – public, private and voluntary – depending on the nature of the emergency. This course of action has been tried and tested, and is considered to be the most effective. It is followed by the military in combat situations with considerable success. The structure encourages innovation and flexibility, and enables operational units to work independently, adapting to the situation as necessary, without the constraint of central control.

The second principle is that the initial response will be raised to whatever level is required to deal with the effects of an emergency and restore normality. The damage has been done, and the public need reassurance. The key to this is to demonstrate that the crisis is being brought under control as far as possible, and the public and the media will be watching to see how this is done. It is important that the highest ranking person steps in to personally minimise the loss.

Contingency arrangements were set up many years ago, allowing central government to activate a regional organisation to assist with the management of civil emergencies in peace time – the Regional Emergency Committees (RECs).

As far as possible the normal administrative arrangements for governing the United Kingdom will be used for coping with an emergency. But if the effects of any emergency are such as to disrupt those arrangements to such a degree that they show signs of becoming ineffective, action will be taken to strengthen them and ensure continuing effectiveness. It is in these circumstances that ministers may consider the activation of one or more of the RECs.

The activation will normally be issued from the Cabinet Office on behalf of the Home Secretary, as Chairman of the Civil Contingencies Unit (CCU). Central government involvement will be managed under the auspices of the CCU.

The CCU is composed of representatives of a number of government departments under the chairmanship of the Secretary of State for the Home Department, assisted by the Head of the Economic and Domestic Affairs Secretariat, Cabinet Office and the Prime Minister's Chief Press Secretary. Its terms of reference are

> To co-ordinate the preparation of plans for ensuring in an emergency the supplies and services essential to the life of the community; to keep these plans under regular review; to supervise their prompt and effective implementation in specific emergencies; and to report as necessary to the appropriate Ministerial Committee.

It is a principle of Integrated Emergency Management that those individuals and organisations responsible for providing services in normal times will be responsible for continuing to do so in the face of an emergency.

All central government departments play a role in overseeing legislation relating to one or more aspects of safety, hazard reduction and emergency planning and management. In the event of a national crisis the government department with the most involvement is pre-nominated as the 'lead department', with the Home Office having the remit of overall responsibility. Lead departments are shown in the current edition of *Dealing with Disaster* (Home Office 1997).

There are nine RECs in England, which are based in the government offices for the regions. There are equivalent emergency committees in Scotland, Wales and Northern Ireland. Once activated, it will be up to each REC chairman (the appropriate government office regional director) to decide how best his/her REC might operate and which organisations should attend its meetings. However, within these general parameters, it is customary for representatives of central government, including the Central Office of Information (COI), to attend as appropriate, and other organisations whose attendance, advice or consultation is required.

Amongst these might be: police, fire, military, telecommunication providers, utilities, local authority chief executives, and some government agencies, such as the Highways Agency. The kind of representation which these organisations might offer would form part of the planning process. As RECs are part of central government, there is no automatic 'right of representation' for any non central government body, and the wishes of the REC chairman are regarded as paramount in this respect.

The REC chairman will be expected to report from time to time to the chairman of the CCU. In addition, representatives of government departments engaged on business with the REC will be expected to report to their parent departments, and industries such as water and gas will be forwarding reports to the headquarters of sponsoring government departments. In this way an overview of the situation in the area covered by the REC will be available to central government to inform discussions.

Once activated, among other duties, RECs will be expected to co-ordinate central government activities in their areas in order to facilitate an effective response to any emergency, with particular reference to maintaining the essentials of life for the community. The REC must act where appropriate as a channel of communication with organisations and authorities engaged in dealing with an emergency and those maintaining essential supplies and services (Home Office 1997). Committees are also responsible for ensuring that information is made publicly available in accordance with government policy, and monitoring the effects of the emergency and the adequacy of the contingency arrangements.

The REC will need to consider the application of priorities decided at the centre to conditions existing in its own area. A decision may be necessary on priorities for the allocation of armed forces manpower and resources to assist the civil authorities, and, in a war emergency, consideration of the allocation of civil resources for service use. These general guidelines would be supplemented by more detailed instructions related to the nature of the emergency at the time the RECs were activated.

For a few emergencies, the initial response will need to start at central government level. This is because the necessary information will first become available at that level. Such emergencies as the

Chernobyl nuclear reactor accident come into this category. Other types of incident which fall into this category would include: nuclear powered and other satellite accidents, widespread industrial action threatening the essentials of life, and war.

It is important to remember that RECs have a co-ordinating and communication role to play in a national crisis. They do not assume the responsibilities of the government departments concerned, or the authorities and organisations with whom individual members of the REC customarily do business. It is conceivable that devolution of the executive authority of government departments might be considered, but the circumstances in which this might happen cannot be forecast.

Generally, industrial troubles affecting a single industry do not need co-ordination at regional level, and may be dealt with through a specialised local committee. It is possible that an escalating industrial action for which a functional group has been activated may subsequently require an REC to be brought into operation, and arrangements will be made to reconcile the relationship between the two.

In an emergency situation affecting fuel and power, sub-committees can be set up in each of the nine government offices for the regions, with separate arrangements for the Welsh Office, the Scottish Office and Northern Ireland. The function of these is to keep the emergency situation under review and ensure that particular needs are identified and met as far as possible. The sub-committee will include industry representatives, and will deal with supply, distribution, marketing, industrial relations and legal matters among other things. In the event of a strike, for example, the committees would be responsible for implementing existing emergency plans, working under powers and the advice of the government. Apart from the CCU and the REC, other major players in a national crisis would include the police, fire and ambulance services.

The armed forces could assume a number of different roles depending on the nature of the crisis. In the Aberfan disaster, when a coal tip slid down the side of a mountain and engulfed the local school, the army assisted in digging through the rubble and helping the civilian authorities. They may be deployed to replace the civil authorities, as in 1969 in Northern Ireland for example, or they could be used as substitute labour during industrial disputes, as in the 1977/8 winter disruption.

Depending on the nature of the emergency, the coastguard, various utilities, telecommunications companies, transport undertakings and other industries might be involved. There are a number of voluntary organisations which may also have a role to play, such as the Red Cross, St John Ambulance, RAYNET, the Women's Royal Voluntary Service and the Salvation Army.

When RECs are activated, the Central Office of Information (COI) is given responsibility to act as information adviser to the chairman in England. This role is fulfilled by the Director of Information Services in Scotland, and the Director of Information in Wales.

Experience has shown that in the event of a major incident or disaster, the demands of the media will put enormous pressure on those responsible for managing the media response. The network offices of the COI are often based in the same building or close to the government offices for the regions, and are staffed by professional press officers who can provide a range of key services. They are experienced in all aspects of media relations, including producing press notices, managing and handling press calls, press pools and public announcements, and organising press conferences. COI staff are available 24 hours a day, and they can be deployed wherever media pressure is stretching local resources to capacity.

There will always be a need to keep the public informed of the action being taken by government and the emergency services in an emergency and the reason for it. It is essential that channels of communication for disseminating government policy and clearing areas of doubt be clearly defined.

There is an immediate need to set up an effective means of communication at or near the site of the disaster. This will operate between the government departments, local authorities and emergency services involved, and the media. COI can help to set up systems and procedures.

As stated at the head of this chapter, a national crisis is a very rare occurrence. It is not possible to live in a totally risk-free environment, and indeed such a state may not be desirable. Integrated Emergency Management principles, by including preparedness, enable us to forecast and analyse potential areas of risk, and prepare physically and psychologically for the unexpected. The organisations involved in emergency planning continue to refine and improve the system, with the aim of ensuring that in the event of a national crisis affecting Great Britain, the emergency services will be able to meet whatever problem faces us and deal with it effectively.

References

Auf der Heide, E. (1989) *Disaster Response: Principles of Preparation and Co-ordination* Baltimore: C. V. Mosby

Berge, D. ten (1988) *The First 24 hours: a comprehensive guide to successful crisis communications* Oxford: Blackwell

Home Office (1997) *Dealing with Disaster* 3rd edition Liverpool: Brodie

Parker, D. and Handmer, J. (1992) *Hazard Management and Emergency Planning: Perspectives on Britain* London: James & James

5 THE LOCAL NEWS

John Jefferson

Try as you might you will be hard pressed to come up with a simpler or more perceptive definition of the differences between local newspapers, television and radio than this one from a most unlikely source, a member of the Women's Institute.

Proposing a vote of thanks to a speaker after his talk about local radio she said: 'When I read my local paper it's like getting a letter from a friend; when I watch my local television station it's like receiving a postcard from a friend; and when I tune in to local radio it's like taking a phone call from a friend'.

This surely sums up the strengths and weakness of each medium and the close relationship which people feel they enjoy with their local media. Each is regarded as a friend. Although people also develop a bond with their favourite national newspaper or their preferred national radio programme such as BBC Radio 4's *Today*, the latter are bound to appear more distant and less in touch than a local media dedicated to telling the daily story of their region.

This is probably less true if you live close to London but as a general rule the further you are from the capital the more successful the local media is likely to be. Its value is measured by what is believed to be the most relevant service to our daily lives.

London is different. National radio stations can feel like local ones in London and local stations see themselves as less parochial and more national in approach. It is difficult to be really local in London because of its size and because London news is often national news anyhow.

If, when the big incident occurs in your patch, you suddenly find yourself operating in the media spotlight, the more you know about how journalism works the better. Although the arrival of national and international news teams poses special problems, their basic needs will be similar to those of your local media – information, interviews, still and moving pictures. Don't forget it is also an opportunity for you and your organisation to shine and to get your message across.

As a start, therefore, it is worthwhile taking a look at your local media to attempt to understand what each does best and, importantly, to appreciate their different deadline pressures, which will indirectly put pressure on you too as a newsmaker.

Local news providers

Local newspapers, particular evening and regional morning papers, have been struggling in recent years with falling circulation and reduced advertising revenue as the competition from radio and television and freebie newspapers intensifies. Nevertheless, they reach a lot of people and they remain an important influence on the lives of the people in the communities they serve.

In spite of the glamour of radio and television – people still find it a thrill to be heard on the wireless or seen on the telly – local decision makers show a respect for what appears in print which radio and television finds it harder to attract. This flattering status is surely linked to a newspaper's role as an instrument of permanent record.

Council leaders remain sensitive to criticism of their policies in the local press and football managers seem to be hurt much more by an adverse review of their team's performance on the back page of a newspaper than an equally critical report on the game during a Saturday afternoon sports programme on local radio.

Once in print, a story is there for posterity and likely to be read and digested by thousands of people. On radio and television a story has its moment and then is usually gone for ever. Local stations offering serious current affairs, debate and documentaries would rightly claim that they too are capable of influencing local thinking and decision-making but on balance newspapers still probably have the edge. Ironically, however, there is some evidence that people are less likely to believe what they read in the press than what they see and hear on television and radio.

When it comes to who is best at delivering news, the real debate begins. Newspapers still have the physical advantage of selling a product which people can hold, read when they want to and can be selective in what they read. Interestingly, at a time when the electronic media industry is moving towards the concept of so-called 'news on-demand' and a news agenda which is bespoke to an individual's needs, a newspaper editor might argue, albeit partly tongue in cheek, that newspapers have been doing just that for years.

In spite of the advantages of immediacy enjoyed by radio and television, their reporting of a major story still seems to act as a billboard for a local paper's coverage. Regardless of the thoroughness of reportage on radio and television, people still appear to want to read it in print for themselves and see the pictures. On a simple word count alone, newspaper coverage will usually be more extensive and comprehensive and fill in details which can be difficult to deal with on-air. They can exploit the advantages of having more thinking time, more journalists lots of space to fill.

Newspaper editors would also take issue at the suggestion that radio and television are most likely to be first with the news. They would point out that it depended on what was meant by 'news'. Once again, they have the time and the staff and the specialist journalists to get to meetings, cultivate contacts and dig out exclusive stories and angles. Most evening newspapers also enjoy the advantage of serving smaller editorial areas, so allowing them to cover stories which, while important, are not important enough to make it on to radio and television prospects lists covering a wider area.

But even the most ardent champion of the local newspaper cause would have to wave the white flag when it comes to considering who will be first when the big news story breaks – not always a major disaster, but a story of considerable interest and relevancy to the local area and probably further afield.

This is the Achilles' heel of the newspaper industry. In the days before local radio and today's extensive regional television news coverage, most daily papers ran many editions from late morning to early evening, with special editions when required so they could handle a breaking story and run with it. Even if the story broke in the evening, there was still the opportunity to clean up the next day.

Today there are usually fewer editions and earlier edition times and editors have to be satisfied in playing a complementary role to radio and television coverage. Although methods of newspaper production have seen much change it remains physically impossible to compete for speed with a live microphones or television cameras.

Since the BBC launched its public service version of local radio, the public has gradually become accustomed to the idea that if you want to find out faster, tune to your local station. Local radio still has the edge, but network radio is hard on its heels and television is getting better all the time at scrambling a live camera to where the action is.

So-called 'rolling news' is a comparatively new idea in the United Kingdom although radio audiences in North America and Australia have long been used to having a local station to which they could turn at any time for information and guidance. The US-based CNN TV channel made the running internationally, with Sky News and more recently, BBC Radio 5 Live being given the credit for developing the philosophy in Britain.

It is a deadline-free zone. Journalists do not have to wait for the next scheduled news bulletin. A rolling, open-ended format of news, current affairs, information and features simply embraces stories as they happen and develops them across the day. Interviews and press conferences are carried live, warts and all, with the viewer and listener watching journalism at work. At the same time they're also watching those running the press conferences at work too.

In practice, BBC local radio has been in the business of 'rolling news' since its inception although the concept had not at that time been given a name. Local radio simply did what came naturally as a result of its flexible programming formats.

A tiny budget and a small staff meant that a station could not offer the type of expensive, heavily produced speech-based programmes such as those provided on Radio 4. Yet, in order to serve its local community properly, it was not sufficient just to play music with a few requests and what's-on items sprinkled amongst the records.

The result was the invention of seamless radio, back to back live sequence programmes capable of carrying news, information and other material within a music framework. Although there were formal news breaks, the opportunities it threw up to broadcast breaking news or urgent information there and then were soon grasped.

A radio car was also part of a station's kit, allowing a station to take its listeners to where the news was being made rather than offering a sanitised recording sometime later or expecting the newsmakers to travel to a studio. Although early radio cars had limited range and reliability and felt only a small evolutionary step away from two cocoa tins and a long piece of string, they were the start of a significant trend in local news coverage.

The usefulness of local radio

The radio's potential as an exclusive source of instant local information was rehearsed in the late sixties by the early stations when power blackouts gave them the chance to broadcast details of which zones within their communities were about to suffer cuts. And stations also exploited other more unlikely information opportunities which had not been thought of before by broadcasters, such as the Lamb Bank on Radio Cumbria – a daily service which linked farmers with ewes which had lost their lambs to farmers with orphaned lambs.

The usefulness of local radio was universally recognised during a particularly bad winter in the early seventies. With local audiences then firmly established and many of the stations enjoying the status of being the most listened to radio service within their communities, they found themselves in the role of central clearing house for information. Hour after hour and day after day, they rotated a mass of details: school and road closures, power cuts, cancelled rail and bus services, and events which were either off or on.

Organisations and individuals heard for themselves what the immediacy of local radio could do for them and their communities in a crisis. Nothing was too trivial: for example, the coal-man with his messages for customers in isolated villages about his efforts to get supplies to them, or the advice to pensioners from the bingo hall manager that they should not attempt to attend that afternoon because the pavements near the hall were too treacherous with snow and ice.

This was way local radio was intended to be. It was offering a platform for the community to talk to itself, with the professional broadcasters working as enablers, and this principle is followed to this day. Listeners all over the country pondered on how they had managed in the days before local radio and one local councillor in Humberside was quoted as saying: 'When war breaks out we turn to the BBC but when it snows we turn to local radio.'

Lessons were also learned at this time about the burden of responsibility resting on the shoulders of local radio staff in ensuring that the public is informed and not misinformed. In one area a station was accused of nearly losing a young woman her job as a secretary. She was an avid listener to the station and heard that the road to the town where she worked was closed so she phoned her office to say she would not be able to report for duty. However, another member of staff, who had not heard the radio message, set off on the same route to the same office and got through. An investigation revealed that the local authority highways staff had opened-up the road and regarded it as 'passable with care' and were also miffed that it had been reported as closed. Understandably, they were anxious to get public recognition for their stalwart efforts to get their community back on the move. The police, however, decided to say the road was closed for fear that it would attract a lot of traffic and that inevitably some vehicles would get stuck and the road would be closed again. They wanted it to be kept clear and available for emergency use only.

This underlines the importance of the emergency services, local authorities and the local media working as a co-ordinated team, but it is an ideal which still remains elusive today.

Elsewhere, a worker anxious for a night off called his local station and convinced the message taker that he was the manager of a local factory and wanted to tell staff that the night shift had been cancelled because of the bad weather. The information went out but fortunately the real manager heard it and a correction was made.

Such experiences also reinforce the message that the service a radio station provides for the public can only be as good as the information supplied. It is a Catch 22 scenario: the local media is most useful to an organisation if it reaches a significant number of people but it will only be able to attract large numbers if the public know the information will be there when they want it.

Nevertheless the public have become educated and accustomed to using local radio as a primary source of information, especially when their community is affected by a major incident. The inherent problems of delivering fast, accurate information remain to be solved by both the providers of information and the broadcasters who pass it on.

A local incident

When a school bus crashed at Wilberfoss, near York, a mother of a pupil at the school involved was on her way home and found herself in the traffic jam caused by the accident. She turned on her car radio to find out what was happening and afterwards had this to say about the experience:

> I was about two minutes away from home when the first report came on the radio that there had been an accident on the 1079. Then gradually further coverage reported that it had been a school bus accident outside Wilberfoss.

> As my son catches a bus home from Pocklington I was obviously quite concerned. During that time further broadcasts were released and at which point I became very worried at some of them. The second one said that it had been a school bus, which I assumed came from Woldgate School, and knowing my son would not have been on the Woldgate bus I was quite relieved. A further broadcast said it had been an East Yorkshire bus with 50 people on board and at that I was very alarmed again because my son travels from Pocklington on an East Yorkshire bus. And when they said people I assumed it was a normal public service bus.

> I feel more positive reporting could be done. It was very worrying for most of us. There were a lot of parents on the road in the traffic diversion. What I think they could have said was where the bus was from, which bus it was and the area to which it was going. I believe there are three buses that use the route to the village of Stamford Bridge. They could at least have said it is a school bus from Woldgate School and it is bus number three, for argument's sake. Would parents of children who travel on that bus please contact this number. Then at least you would reduce the amount of people wanting to ring the hospitals, the police and the school. And instead of having 1400 to 1600 parents going absolutely out of their minds with worry you could have limited it down to 50 people.

Radio station editors would echo those sentiments. It underpins their view that emergency services, local authorities and other organisations could help themselves and others by helping us to do a better job. However, in the emotion and confusion surrounding a major incident there are genuine difficulties standing in the way of making available more detailed and accurate information at the speed at which she suggests. The system is not geared up to deliver this, and maybe it should be.

BBC local radio is of course only one of the players. There are some 37 BBC stations providing coverage across every English county as well as the Channel Islands. In Scotland, Wales and Northern Ireland the BBC operates some very local stations, but for the most part it delivers its 'localness' through regional radio.

The Radio Authority on the other hand now oversees more than 200 independent (commercial) radio (IR) stations across the UK. Together they attract significant audiences and all carry news and information to a lesser or greater extent. Each IR station is different and they vary from big city stations to small community stations run by volunteers. Whilst it is unthinkable that any of them would ignore a major incident it is impossible to summarise how they might want to respond. This is likely to be governed by the extent to which they will be willing to disrupt their music schedules and whether they have the resources to process a mass of information.

The last few years have seen a growth in the number of localised news bulletins on both BBC and ITV. Local news on television used to confine itself to weekday evenings but now we see local windows within national television breakfast shows and bulletins across the day and at weekends. ITV in some areas has found ways to provide sub-regional editions of its news programmes whereas the BBC operates mostly on a regional basis.

The other crucial development has been the provision of small, highly mobile television outside broadcast vehicles at regional centres. Local television news programmes now find it much easier to carry live on-site reports into their bulletins and frequently anchor part or all of a programme from where the news is being made.

The local radio car still wins the race to be first on-air. All it requires is a journalist who can drive. The television van is bulkier and needs more specialist crewing but it will not be far behind.

Other radio strengths are its portability, the ability of radios to run on batteries when power supplies fail, which could be crucial in certain circumstances, and the ease and speed with which programmes can be accessed when information of urgent public interest needs to be broadcast. Local radio stations enjoy the autonomy of being able to respond to community needs, day and night. Regional BBC and ITV stations are entwined within national networks so it is much more tricky, although not impossible, to abandon scheduled programmes.

These are still early days for the new media players: cable, with its potential for city-based television; and Internet style on-line services which enable users to select the news they want, when they want it, in text, audio and video. The latter are, in effect, super versions of Ceefax and Teletext. Whilst they will eventually revolutionise the way we get our information, they are still at the embryo stage. However, at least one big city newspaper in the United States used the Internet recently to break an exclusive story. The report missed its last edition and, fearing the story would leak out to local radio and television, the editor chose to run it on the paper's Internet page some 12 hours before its next edition.

Getting to know the local media

The development of small community radio and television stations and the lure of unrestricted publishing opportunities on the Internet, may well mean that the media pack will be joined in the future by news hounds with less training and experience and less traditional thinking and caution. This should to send a shiver down the backs of those who might be involved in crisis and disaster planning and who are already nervous about working with the media. It may not seem like it at times, but most of the journalists you are likely to have dealings with currently will have been formally trained, and represent news gathering organisations with reputations they are keen to retain.

On the other hand, on-line services could also be exploited by those dealing with a crisis or disaster themselves, allowing them direct access to the public to say what they want to say and thus by-pass the established media.

To a lesser extent local radio and television offers a similar opportunity to spokespersons. If you are interviewed by the local press you have to rely on the reporter correctly interpreting what you have said and identifying what is important and relevant. The latter also applies if you elect to pre-record an interview for radio or television. If, on the other hand, you agree to appear live on radio or television, you can say precisely what you want to say – interviewer permitting, of course.

It is worth noting that different times of day offer different types of opportunity on local radio. If you are invited to participate by phone or in the studio during the breakfast show the format is only likely to allow you a maximum of five or six minutes to get your message over. The audience has a short attention span at that time of day but it is probably the biggest of the broadcasting day. If the interview is scheduled for later in the morning or afternoon, it could last from ten minutes to half an hour and even longer if you are prepared to take phone calls.

Anyone who, in the course of their work, is required to talk to the press and be interviewed on local radio and television, ought to take the time to establish media contacts. Get to know the editor, news editor and feature editor of the local paper and if there is a freelance news agency in your area who supply the national press, meet the people running it.

BBC regional centres are bi-media operations, that is, they cover radio and television, and each is run by a Head of Centre, in effect the Editor in Chief. The regional television bit of the operation has an editor and so has each local radio station. Try to meet them and their senior news producers and news editors. Commercial television and radio stations vary their structures but if there is a news room there is likely to be a news editor or similar and there will probably be a local or group programme controller too.

If you haven't seen the inside of a television or radio studio, ask to be shown around so that when you make your first appearance you are not overwhelmed by the mass of technical equipment surrounding you. It is also enlightening to sit in on a live television or radio news programme to experience for yourself how it is put together and the pressures staff are working under. It is even worth inquiring about the possibility of a dry run television or radio interview so as to experience what it is like before the real thing.

Journalists have differing views about that kind of exercise. Some believe that, because the local media relies so heavily on members of the local community being prepared to face the microphone and hopefully making a good job of it, it is perfectly justifiable to offer them basic training in how to set about it. Others, particularly if politicians are involved, worry about the editorial morality of training people in techniques which help them to field difficult questions.

And don't forget the specialist journalists too. You will find them working on larger daily newspapers and within BBC regions. They cover subjects such as local government, community affairs, education, health, transport and the environment.

On a day-to-day basis, of course, you are more likely to have to work with a reporter fresh out of journalism college. The local media does tend to be a training ground and this lack of experience can stretch your confidence in the person's ability to grasp the story and produce an accurate account. This is another reason for establishing contacts at a more senior level. Junior reporters at the start of their careers come and go but news editors and editors hang around for longer.

As in every other walk of life, networking is very effective in building up productive relationships. It is not a question of having an editor's ear so that you can pull strings. Don't even think about it! But senior local journalists have the interests of their community at heart and they wish to retain its trust. It is not in their interest to get things wrong, so background briefings can be extremely useful.

In a crisis situation in which it may be difficult for all the right reasons to give out certain information, a call to senior journalist contacts explaining the problem may be helpful to all concerned. There are already agreed procedures in place for dealing with sensitive issues such as hostage taking where media coverage might endanger life.

There is an important bonus in getting to know the local media movers and shakers. They are the people who on a daily basis tip off the national media and often supply the words, tapes and pictures used by national newspapers, television and radio.

Should a major incident occur, the locals will be first on the scene and although their principal purpose ought to be to serve their local audience they will also hold the fort for the nationals until reinforcements arrive. Local radio and television editors have a responsibility to feed the network news rooms so they should be happy to advise you on the kind of extra provision required for additional satellite vehicles, camera points and so on.

In addition, BBC News bases television and radio correspondents at some of its regional centres so it could be worthwhile putting them on your visiting list too. Sky News also has its own regional reporters. They are the ones most likely to be telling your story to a national and even international audience.

The picture that emerges therefore is of a local media which by and large complements each other's strengths and weaknesses and the more you know about how they work the more confidence you are likely to have in your dealings with them.

A plane crashes

To illustrate how this complex media machine speeds into action and the pressures it places on operational staff involved in an emergency, let us look at what happened when a small commuter plane crashed in a field near the North Yorkshire village of Dunkeswick in May 1995, killing all 12 people on board, and how the tragedy was covered by local radio and television. A timetable showing the BBC coverage of the incident is given in Table 4.

It happened in the early evening whilst BBC local radio news programmes in West Yorkshire and North Yorkshire were still on the air. Local ITV news programmes were about to begin and there was just over half an hour to go to the start of the BBC's regional news programme, *Look North*, in Leeds. It was also a time of intense activity within the news rooms of the national dailies and the regional morning paper, the *Yorkshire Post*. On BBC1 the 6.00 news was about to start and the main 9.00 national bulletin was only three hours away.

The Knight Air flight took off from Leeds-Bradford airport at 5.46 p.m. bound for Aberdeen. At 5.50 it disappeared off the radar screen and six minutes later the emergency services received a 999 call saying the plane had gone down in a field some distance from a main road. By 6.00 North Yorkshire police, fire and rescue, and ambulance services were mobilised.

At 6.07 the West Yorkshire police press office was alerted to the incident, although the crash happened just over the West Yorkshire border. Minutes later the same press office received a call from a local newspaper reporter saying he understood there had been an accident and almost simultaneously came a call from the BBC news room in Leeds following a tip off. At 6.15 a press officer with the North

Yorkshire police was called into the force control room to handle media calls. News of the crash was flashed by BBC Radio Leeds at 6.30 and ten minutes later the station carried an interview with an emergency services spokesperson. During this same period BBC Radio York, which covers North Yorkshire, also broadcast the first news of the incident after being alerted by the Leeds news room. *Look North* flashed the news and committed two minutes at the end of the programme to report what it knew. It eventually featured an interview with North Yorkshire Fire Brigade in this slot.

During this same time span, West Yorkshire police was receiving calls from all over the country and they were referred to North Yorkshire police. At the same time the senior police officer designated to assume the role of incident commander was making his way to the scene and arrived at 6.45. By then, more than 20 emergency personnel were there and eleven bodies had been located. He was also confronted by half a dozen media representatives.

The BBC in Leeds had already notified its London colleagues and news of the crash was flashed on BBC 1 at 7.00. During the next half hour BBC radio and television reporters and camera teams arrived at the incident with radio car and television satellite vehicles. Other BBC reporters and vehicles were sent to Leeds-Bradford airport.

At 7.30 the incident commander returned from the crash site to establish a command point, the twelfth body having been found. By now there were some 60 media people milling around and in danger of straying onto the crash site and he promised a briefing within 15 minutes.

At 7.45 it was announced that there was to be a press conference at the airport and at 7.57 the police issued a telephone number for relatives to call.

In practice it was some 50 minutes later before the incident commander, along with a senior fire officer, felt able to talk to the press. He confirmed that there were believed to be 12 fatalities and no survivors. Some photographers and cameramen requested closer access to the scene and, after agreeing pooling arrangements, some were allowed further forward. He promised a further press briefing and also put in a request for a press officer to be sent to the scene to help him cope with the intense media interest.

Time	Activity
5.46	Knight Air flight takes off from Leeds-Bradford airport
5.50	Flight disappears from radar screens
5.56	Emergency services receive 999 call from member of public
6.00	N. Yorks. emergency services mobilised
6.07	W. Yorks. police press office alerted
6.08	W. Yorks. police press office receives calls from *Yorkshire Post* and BBC Radio Leeds after tip-off
6.15	N. Yorks. press officer called into force information room
6.30–7.00	News flashed on BBC Radios Leeds and York, *Look North* and BBC1. Radio and TV phone interviews with emergency services
6.45	N. Yorks. police incident commander arrives on scene. 6 media reps already there
7–8.00	Live reports from scene on BBC Radios Leeds and York
7.30	60 media reps now present. Incident commander promises press briefing
7.57	N. Yorks. police release telephone number for relatives to call
8.20	Incident commander and senior fire officer give press briefing
8.30	First press briefing message on N. Yorks. police Media Line
8.50	First TV pictures from the scene arrive at BBC in Leeds
9.00	Lead story on BBC1 *Nine O'Clock News*
9.25	News bulletin ends with live interviews and reports from Leeds-Bradford airport and accident scene
9.28	BBC regional TV bulletin: further live coverage from both outside broadcast points
10.15	Incident commander, senior fire and police officers hold second press briefing
10.30	Further live coverage on BBC2 *Newsnight*

Table 4 Plane crash: timetable of events

At 8.30 the first recorded press message became available on North Yorkshire police's 'Media Line'.

The first pictures of the scene arrived at the BBC in Leeds at 8.50 and were included in a report on the accident at the start of the *Nine O'Clock News*. The bulletin ended at 9.25 with a live interview with a representative of Knight Air at Leeds-Bradford airport and a live report from the crash site. The regional bulletin which followed carried further live coverage.

At 9.40 a press officer from West Yorkshire police arrived at Dunkeswick to help the incident commander prepare for a second press conference. At 10.15 the second press briefing was held, and repeated requests from the media to be allowed to the crash site were denied. By 1030 the BBC *Newsnight* programme was on the air with more live coverage.

For the incident commander it was an experience he will never forget. It was a dark, wet night and the plane had come down in a barley field. Access to it was via a narrow country lane and over a ploughed field. When he arrived the lane was blocked by emergency and media vehicles. The site was potentially the scene of a crime so his duty and priority was to secure it. The number of media people was growing all the time and he was anxious to gain their co-operation and stop them attempting to get to the wreckage. Communications from the scene were difficult and hindered his attempts to confirm how many people had been on board the aircraft.

As he prepared for the press conference and in the absence of advice from a professional press officer, he agonised over whether he should say there had been no survivors in the knowledge that he may be broadcasting live into the homes of the relatives of the victims.

With hindsight, he did a commendable job, recognised the need to provide information for the media and did his best under very difficult circumstances to deliver. Whether assistance from a press officer should have been called for earlier is a matter for debate but it does serve as another example of the size of the burden on operational staff if they are expected to deal with a complex incident and host the media at the same time.

6 THE LOCAL CRISIS

John Jefferson

The local media has a unique role to play in the management of a major emergency within their community. Used intelligently, they can provide a direct link into the homes of the community and so deliver vital information, advice and reassurance.

Experience suggests, however, that organisations under pressure tend to see the media as a single entity and a huge burden to be borne and don't always spot that local radio and regional television and local and regional newspapers offer important opportunities too. The response is reactive rather than proactive.

When the big story breaks, public relations and press officers working in the emergency services, local government and industry appear, understandably, to be anxious to be seen to be fair to all and there is a nervousness about responding to demands from the local media for special treatment. In any case, those same press officers will usually claim that they have good day-to-day relationships with local journalists, understand their needs and suggest politely that you are preaching to the converted. They perceive the bigger challenge during an emergency to be the arrival en masse of the national and international media.

In practice, it is rare when the heat is on for those cosy day-to-day arrangements to be robust enough to deliver what is required by local colleagues. Special treatment may be difficult if that is taken to imply favouring the locals at the expense of the visitors, but recognition of their special role and what is wanted ought to be a priority if a community is to be properly informed.

Whilst all local journalists would rightly claim to be able to offer a conduit through which you can communicate with the local community in such circumstances, it is local radio and to a lesser extent regional television who would lay claim to the advantages of immediacy. As local television and localised on-line Internet-style services develop, they too will be in the business of instant news and information. Newspapers, during the early stages of a major incident, are restricted by their edition times and the delay in getting papers out into the streets and homes.

This chapter refers mostly to BBC local radio because it is speech-based and because of its traditional public service role. Its main business remains news and information. Most commercial operators offer pure music stations catering for specific sections of the music market. That's their business so they carry much less news and information and have smaller news teams. But they do reach audiences which BBC stations don't, especially younger people, and should not be ignored as an outlet for information. The best advice is to make contact with your local commercial station and find out what it can offer.

When the story breaks

The growth of local radio over the past 30 years and the ability now of regional television stations to be quickly on the scene of an incident and beam back live pictures, means that the public in the nineties expects to tune in and to be able to find out immediately and accurately what is happening when a big story breaks within their area.

Although local radio at a time of local crisis is gathering material for its news bulletins like the rest of the media, it also believes that it has another important role to play in passing on vital information such as advice, guidance and reassurance during the first critical hour or two. This is particularly true of incidents involving large fires, explosions and chemical leakage when there is the likelihood of life threatening air or river pollution.

So why is it that when a major incident occurs, the local media still finds it so difficult to get its hands quickly on the information which it believes the public want? It is certainly not for the want of trying and for the most part it is not because organisations involved are unwilling to co-operate.

A simple explanation is that those involved directly in dealing with an incident are so busy coping that the last thought on their minds is the media. Their press officers swing into action but usually remain at their office desk and find it almost as difficult to get information from the scene as the media journalists themselves.

The machinery which deals so effectively with day-to-day media inquiries becomes incapable of delivering information to local stations at the speed at which it is required.

Systems still too often appear to be geared to the less pressurised deadlines of the local press who, unless news breaks right on edition time, can afford to wait for a fuller picture of the incident to emerge and for information to start flowing. One wonders why, in this multi-media age, some PR folk still inhabit 'Press Offices' and not 'Media Relations Departments'. It is just a name but maybe it sends out the wrong vibes.

Or could it be that too many press officers and the senior officers in the emergency services and local government have simply failed to think out how they might use the local media in a more proactive way to communicate with the public? Why just rely on the policeman with the hand held loudhailer when they could have direct access to the airwaves and that great loudhailer in the sky – the wireless?

One of the problems is that every incident is different and thankfully catastrophes do not hit communities very often. During any incident many lessons are learned and everyone vows to do better next time but when the next time comes the emergency workers have changed and so have the journalists so it is back to square one.

One sympathises with those trying to serve the media. Suddenly, resources designed for a normal daily workload of inquiries are expected to stretch to accommodate the big one and they won't.

Perhaps it is also a simple matter of logistics. Assuming that the local media receive an early tip-off, reporters will get to an incident just about as fast as the police and fire brigade, as we saw in the previous chapter. Within minutes they can be broadcasting live on radio via a mobile phone or radio car. It is also becoming increasingly common to find a television outside broadcast vehicle on the scene almost as quickly, with its potential for live pictures and reports. Perhaps the media are asking for the impossible if they expect the senior police or fire officers to make themselves available for interview when they are still assessing the situation and attempting to deal with its complexities and the saving of lives.

Nonetheless, this is the way media coverage is going and whether such unyielding demands are reasonable or not is irrelevant. It is a fact of modern life so those responsible for providing information need to acknowledge it and, if necessary, take their arrangements for media provision back to the drawing board.

Once the news breaks that a major incident has occurred, local radio will endeavour to serve its listeners' needs with or without the co-operation of the authorities involved. Everyone wants to be first with the news although the BBC and other responsible news gathering organisations would say that it is better to be second and right than first and wrong. But that is not to say that responsible journalists should sit by the telephone and do nothing for two hours and wait for a press release to be issued. You can imagine what the public would think about a radio station which flashed news of an emergency but then failed to supply any information about it.

A radio station has to show excellent judgement when faced with such a predicament. It must tease out as much reliable information as it can from as many sources as it can in an attempt to build a picture for its audience. As during severe weather, the station will become a clearing house for information as the public and organisations call in with their contributions. To fulfil this role without the key players is difficult and even dangerous, with a high risk of confusing the public and even causing unnecessary alarm and panic. For the most part, local journalists and their families live within the community so there can be a feeling of personal involvement.

A radio station, like all other media outlets, jealously guards its editorial independence. But most radio station editors and controllers believe they can be at their most effective at a time of crisis if they work in partnership with the communities they serve. That usually means that they will be co-operative in offering the microphone to those charged with dealing with the emergency so that they can have direct access to the public. They are the ones best equipped to give guidance and reassurance, not radio presenters and reporters.

The remainder of this chapter takes you through the coverage by a BBC local radio station of a serious fire at a factory in 1992. It illustrates some of these issues and gives an idea of some of the problems faced by the local media in trying to report on an incident when no-one is available to give information.

The Allied Colloids factory fire

There was a history of concern by local residents about this Bradford factory and the chemicals stored there. At 2.20 p.m. on Tuesday 21 July 1992, their worst nightmares came true. A series of explosions led to a severe fire breaking out in a storeroom.

A reporter in the BBC Radio Leeds news room in Bradford spotted the thick black smoke which resulted, and an immediate enquiry to the emergency services enabled the station to broadcast the brief facts that a fire and explosion had occurred.

Reporters and the radio car were despatched to the factory and to the local hospital so as to give the station an early indication of any casualties. In the central news room in Leeds, other staff were ringing the emergency services and local authority to see what additional information they could glean.

The 3.00 bulletin led with the news although information was still difficult to come by. The report explained that there had been an explosion and a fire and that a huge plume of thick black smoke was billowing out over the area. Some listeners had reported that there were 'black blobs falling out of the sky'. There were some details about the number of fire appliances attending the incident.

During the next hour, the station's main priority was to find someone who would offer the public guidance as to what they should do about the smoke and whether it was likely to be toxic. Ideally, it would have been a police or fire brigade spokesman who would have been prepared to go on air or, as second best, their guidance could have been passed on by the presenter. By the 4.00 bulletin there was little that journalists could add to the story and a sense of frustration was building up at the station.

By this time a number of listeners had called in to seek advice. They were told to contact their local police station but complained that the number was always engaged.

Shortly after 4.00, a concerned caller who could see the smoke, spoke on the telephone to the programme presenter.

Caller Well at the moment I can see clouds of smoke which keep drifting across and now and then it dies down a bit and then it gathers momentum and gets thicker and blacker and we are all getting a bit worried.

Presenter When did you first see the smoke?

Caller About half past two. We thought it was a bonfire or something. Then it got thicker and it smells a bit like sulphur. We looked out of the bedroom window and saw that Allied Colloids was burning and it's been going strong ever since then.

Presenter Have you been able to get any information other than from Radio Leeds?

Caller I rang the local police first of all and asked them if they knew anything about it and they just said that there is a fire at Allied Colloids and to stay in and keep the windows closed, which we already were doing, but even now there are people wandering around and children playing out so nobody seems to be telling us what to do.

This prompted a call from a Bradford Councillor who was also put on the air.

Presenter Traffic and travel-wise, well the main message has got to be to stay away from the area affected by the fire. Bradford Met have told us that their Bradford Dewsbury [bus] service, the number 268, has been diverted due to the fire. Cleckheaton Road has been closed so the service is being diverted. There are also delays on the Huddersfield Road, all services there are likely to experience delays. A Bradford city councillor who lives near the factory is on the line now. What can you see?

Caller Some very dark smoke out of my door.

Presenter How close are you to the fire?

Caller About 400 yards.

Presenter So you are in the area where people should be told if there is any danger?

Caller This is why I rang you because as far as I am concerned the procedures have been carried out where I live.

Presenter And those procedures are what?

Caller We were all told by the police – they've been down where I live three times – to close your windows and go upstairs.

Presenter What is it like, because I understand you have been out before you were told to stay indoors?

Caller I actually set off to try to get to a meeting at City Hall at half two and I turned round when I realised what was happening. The road wasn't closed off then and I turned round because I have three cats which were outside and I came home to put them in.

Presenter So what is the situation now – you have thick very black smoke outside your door?

Caller Yes, it's very frightening.

One of the reporters who had had been collating information in the news room now had sufficient material to go on air. Fortunately, he was an experienced hand with good local knowledge and was able to draw upon this to fill in the gaps.

Presenter What has been the response from the emergency services?

Reporter As far as we know the alert came very quickly. There are well known procedures for dealing with these kind of incidents and I believe that at Allied Colloids there are some on-site fire fighting facilities.

Presenter What about the local people, how many people have been told to stay in and close windows?

Reporter This isn't clear at this stage but the emergency procedure requires a certain area around the factory to be sealed off so the initial response from the company I would assume would be to alert local people to any danger there may be.

Presenter We are just hearing from the National Rivers Authority that they are warning people to keep clear of the Low Moor Beck and River Spen because of a pollution threat. From your monitoring of the situation how much of a problem is this fire causing?

Reporter As we have been hearing the traffic problems in the area will be immense because the road that runs past Allied Colloids runs to the main Odsal roundabout which is one of the main thoroughfares in the city of Bradford. Many people use it as an alternative to the M606 so any time, day or night, there is always plenty of traffic there and at twenty past four the traffic problems will be quite severe.

Then, after 4.30, a breakthrough: the station was able to contact the chief executive of Bradford City Council.

Presenter We return now to our main story. Joining me is Bradford's chief executive. What is the latest information you have?

Chief Executive Well we are still awaiting confirmation of just how serious this incident is. What we've done in line with our emergency planning scheme is to establish a control centre here in City Hall where, as it happens, from the room I am in, I can see the smoke coming out of Allied Colloids and drifting across the city. We've got various council services on standby; we have an arrangement with our sports centre at Odsal to receive evacuees and so on and we've got our school welfare transport available to take evacuees to that centre if necessary. I have to emphasise that no-one has been evacuated yet. Our latest information from the police, it's a bit hazy, is that they don't think this is toxic smoke.

Then it was the turn of one of the reporters at the scene with the radio car.

Presenter What's the latest situation as far as you are concerned?

Reporter I am as near as the police will allow anyone to get to the fire, which is about 300 yards, and we can still feel the heat from that far away. If anything, the fire looks as though it's getting worse. There is thick black smoke billowing into the sky and the occasional fireball exploding. It is a very worrying and very dramatic sight and I am sure one that can be seen from most parts of Bradford. It has completely blocked out the sky on one side of the factory. It reminds me of pictures from the Gulf War – all one can see is blackness, no light is getting through at all.

Presenter It seems it is very hard to get hold of information, presumably everyone is at the scene and not able to help provide information for us and the rest of the media?

Reporter That's right, it is literally all hands to the pumps.

The 5.00 bulletin added little more to the story but shortly afterwards it was back to the council's emergency control room.

Chief Executive Our understanding is that things are under control. We have had it confirmed that the smoke coming out of this fire is not toxic. It is unpleasant and is resulting in quite a lot of complaints about black blobs of stuff landing in different parts of the district but our environmental health people are looking at those and I don't think there is any danger to life or limb. As far as we are concerned we are standing by. We have that line of school buses waiting at the sports centre. We are planning to keep the alert going probably until six o'clock when we expect another update from the emergency services, after which time I will stand down my people.

Meanwhile anxious calls continued to be made to the radio station from people in the area. This woman lived 100 yards from the factory.

Caller The flames are still billowing but the smoke has cleared. We are not allowed to go back into our houses, we are not really being told anything, we are just stood around waiting to see.

Presenter Are you unhappy with the way you have been treated this afternoon as regards the lack of information?

Caller All I can see is all I know. We have been asking the policemen what they know but they are not telling us very much because I feel they don't know.

Presenter We have just heard that a number of people have been taken to Bradford Royal Infirmary suffering from eye problems, including a local resident, a policeman and two firemen.

Then, some three and a half hours after the fire started, the station finally managed to get someone from the emergency services on to the air.

Presenter It is now 12 minutes to six o'clock and in a few moments we will be talking to a chemist about chemicals and their dangers but before that we'll talk to a senior fire officer. How has the fire service responded to this incident today?

Fire officer We've had 25 fire engines, many specialist appliances and over 150 fire fighters here.

Presenter Where would you put it on the scale of emergencies?

Fire Officer It was an extremely large fire with many very flammable and toxic materials and we have had two large buildings involved. But I would say that although there is a large quantity of very nasty looking smoke we still believe that there is no substantial danger to residents in the area provided they stay indoors and keep their doors and windows closed.

Presenter How long is it likely to last?

Fire Officer We will certainly be here all night. We have the fire surrounded but there is still a lot of fuel burning and we will have to continue to apply large quantities of water to keep it safe.

And then it was the turn of the company spokesman for Allied Colloids, someone the radio station would have preferred to have heard from much earlier.

Presenter What actually caused the incident?

Company spokesman As far as we are able to ascertain at the moment the fire started in our raw materials warehouse. I heard the earlier conversation about the toxic nature of the chemicals. Clearly we do handle a wide variety of chemicals but the raw materials warehouse involved, although it is our main warehouse for material which comes in, in bags et cetera, our major raw materials are held elsewhere and they, together with our production facilities, are unaffected.

Presenter Have safety regulations failed?

Company spokesman No I don't believe they have failed. We are certainly very pleased with the way the emergency procedures have been activated and of course the fire authorities have done a magnificent job in attending to us.

Presenter Should workers be turning up tonight?

Company spokesman No, our instructions at the moment to our workforce is not to turn up for work at the moment but, because our production facilities are largely unaffected, and subject to electric power being available, we hope to be back in production very quickly.

So what went wrong?

Radio Leeds enjoyed a good working relationship with West Yorkshire police and fire brigade, so why did that relationship fail to deliver the goods that afternoon? Was Radio Leeds guilty of over-reacting to an incident, expecting too much and trying too hard to quarry information which simply wasn't available?

It became clear after the Health and Safety Executive published its report on the incident that for some hours the police and fire brigade had to deal with difficult issues and a quite confusing situation. There were problems in finding a water supply, the on-going threat of the fire spreading to other chemicals and a delay in sounding the company's emergency siren which was then silenced when the power supply was cut off to the site.

There was considerable uncertainty about the nature of the smoke and whether it was toxic. It was in fact a burning cocktail of over 400 chemicals and it would have been impossible to confirm the constituent materials and confirm or allay public fears.

The police were not alerted until 2.28 p.m. and by 3.17 had asked for public address cars which arrived a few minutes later and toured the area warning residents to stay inside and close all windows and doors. Eight properties close to the warehouse were evacuated and a larger scale evacuation was considered. Dense smoke from the blaze also caused rush hour traffic problems on nearby service roads and on the M606 and M62.

No-one was injured at the factory but 33 people were taken to Bradford Royal Infirmary, including 20 firemen and police officers. Six were admitted and kept in overnight. A local disabled resident suffered an acute asthma attack and was admitted to hospital for a week.

Sticky deposits fell up to 400 metres from the site and soot particles were found 10 kilometres away. During the days that followed there were warnings not to eat fruit or vegetables grown in the area and to avoid a local stream which had become contaminated.

Time	Activity
2.20	Series of explosions leading to a fire
2.28	Arrival of first fire appliances
2.32	Police dispatched to the scene
2.45	Smoke and calls from public alert Bradford council's environmental health officers; initial arrangements made for large scale evacuation
2.45	BBC Radio Leeds enquiry to emergency services re smoke; first news flash
2.55	Allied Colloids emergency siren sounded
3.22	Police public address cars warn nearby residents to stay indoors
3.40	Emergency siren stops when power to site is cut off
3–4.00	Main story on radio bulletin; information limited to basic details. AA road watch reports on traffic hold ups. Listeners call radio station for advice
4–4.30	Radio station interviews on-air listener eye witnesses, including a councillor whose home is affected; National Rivers Authority put out pollution warning via local radio; first live news report from scene by telephone
4.35	Live interview with city's chief executive at emergency control centre; first live radio car report from scene
5.10	City's chief executive progress report indicating emergency may be over by 6.00
5.20	News of people being taken to Bradford Royal Infirmary
5.40	Fire contained
5.50	Senior fire officer radio interview
5.55	Allied Colloids spokesman interviewed on radio

Table 5 Factory fire: timetable of events

Clearly it was a major incident. Staff at BBC Radio Leeds remain convinced that they were justified in pursuing the story as they did and believe that the station, the emergency services and the factory failed between them to deliver information the public had a right to expect.

As in other similar incidents elsewhere, there was no question of those involved being bloody minded or deliberately unco-operative. Those close to the incident were so busy getting on with the task that no-one was thinking strategically about what they should be saying to the public and how the media might be even be helpful allies.

Whilst it is uncommon these days for police officers to adopt a 'tell 'em nowt' stance, one suspects there is still a nervousness to go on air unless the full facts are available. Perhaps there is a feeling that to admit to not knowing the answer to a key question – for example, is the smoke toxic? – is likely to reflect badly on both them and the force.

In this new age of instant radio and television coverage, a different attitude is needed and the public deserve to be treated as grown ups. Radio Leeds would have liked early access to a police spokesperson who would have shared with the public what was *not* known as well as what was known. Bradford's chief executive did just that and the effect was to give the public confidence that their local authority was on top of the situation.

Listeners would surely have understood why it was impossible to determine the toxicity of the smoke if some explanation had been given of the complex nature of the problem, coupled with reassurance that expert assessment was underway to try to come up with an answer. The advice to stay indoors which was being broadcast by police cars in the neighbourhood could also have been repeated for the benefit of the wider radio audience along with other factual details about what the police and fire brigade were doing to safeguard lives and property.

The Allied Colloids experience also poses a question about where press officers ought to base themselves at such a time – in their office at the end of a phone or at the incident. The answer is probably both and that may then become an issue of staffing levels. There were measures aplenty at Allied Colloids for keeping reporters away from the scene but no-one there to assist them.

If an organisation is seriously committed to improving its media arrangements in an emergency, this is arguably the most crucial area for improvement.

When an incident occurs reporters and camera operators will automatically head for the scene whilst others make phone calls. Common sense dictates that someone experienced in media relations needs to be there from the start to handle the media and allow operational officers to get on with their jobs. This implies that the media relations expert is also senior enough to have the clout to ensure that information is forthcoming and to insist that someone of seniority is available for interview.

Journalists still prefer to interview those in charge rather than a public relations professional, but a senior officer freed from having to handle demands for basic information, camera vantage points and so on may be more inclined to break off briefly to talk into a microphone. Company executives also seem rarely to be proactive in such matters and yet they have much to lose in terms of the public image of their organisations. Practicalities get in the way of efforts by journalists to track them down. When a major incident occurs the company involved has a lot on its plate and it is usually impossible to get through on the telephone or bypass the police cordon physically to search them out.

The people of Bradford may well have thought more highly of Allied Colloids if a spokesperson had taken the initiative earlier in the afternoon to talk to the radio station and offer the public some insight into the problems it was facing.

When the dust settles

So far, we have concentrated on the so-called 'mayhem' stage, the chaotic early part of an incident. Once this is over, the dust settles and the smoke drifts away, the media inquest begins into exactly what happened, why it happened and who was to blame. Immediacy is no longer important so the local press is back in business and operating on a more level playing field.

Newspapers will feature maps and diagrams and expert analysis, and local television may well go down the same route but in much less detail. Local radio will want to be heard to be asking the right people the right questions and to be opening up the issue to public debate through phone ins and discussion.

During the mayhem period interviews are likely to be fact-finding based on the who, what, where, when and how school of interviewing. Later the questioning is likely to tougher, challenging and probably political.

Phone ins are often criticised as cheap and nasty radio, and some are. But properly chaired and produced they can offer the public a unique platform from which to vent their feelings. They can also act as an emotional release if an incident has left a community in trauma. The day after Dunblane, local stations across the country found that people were desperate to talk about it, to express their anger and sorrow: to get it out of their system, if you like.

One thing is for sure, long after the national and international media circus has left town, the local media will continue to pursue a story and the issues it has raised. It will rumble on until the community itself signals it has read and heard enough.

7 COMMUNICATING IN AN INTERNATIONAL EMERGENCY: NORTHERN IRAQ FROM 1991

Tom Hardie-Forsyth

This chapter is a personal appraisal of the way the quality of and commitment to communication could determine, sometimes fatally, the handling of complex emergencies. It draws mainly upon my experiences in northern Iraq, both initially (in 1991) as an army officer with the British contingent of the Safe Haven operation and subsequently (from 1991–5) in my work with voluntary agencies and others in the region.

The one thing that struck me forcibly as I delved more and more deeply into my own experience and the experiences of others who took part in this operation, was the paradoxical disparity between the effectiveness that was achieved in our technical communications and the often correspondingly desultory performance in our communication with each other in the wider human sense. I include in this rather sombre appraisal that of inter-agency communication. I have come to the firm conclusion that a key element in this problem was the difficulty that agencies and individuals found themselves in when attempting to communicate across substantial cultural barriers.

When I use the word cultural, I am not referring to the word in its ethnic sense, but in its broader generic sense; thus including organisational cultures, prejudices and sometimes simply good old 'need-to-know' bloody-mindedness (something which seems especially to afflict governmental and international agencies).

There is no attempt in this chapter to claim the dignity of academic rigour. Indeed rather than being a cogent development, leading to postulated solutions, it is more in the form of a series of snap shots; some grainy, some quite sharply focused and all, as far as I am concerned, very real and containing within them the germ of some crucial lessons in how we should (and shouldn't) communicate with one another when dealing with complex emergency situations. If the reader detects a hint of barely suppressed anger in my writing – good. I offer no apologies. For when human lives are at risk, politeness does not appear high in my list of priorities.

To bring some structure into this chapter I am going to divide it into what I think are its five natural sections:

1. Political/military communication

2. Military communication with Non-Governmental Organisations (NGOs)

3. Communication between NGOs

4. Communication between all agencies and the local population

5. Communication with the media

But before I do this, I will just briefly set the scene and describe my own role.

I am sure most readers will remember the basic situation that led to Operation Safe Haven amongst the Kurdish population in northern Iraq. Towards the end of the Gulf conflict there was an uprising of local populations in Iraq in both the north and south of the country; the northern uprising being mainly Kurdish in nature. Setting aside the politics and the history of these uprisings, by the middle of March of 1991 they had failed disastrously and in the north of the country hundreds of thousands of people began to flee from the avenging Iraqi forces into the mountains on both the Turkish and Iranian borders. The physical conditions at the time were absolutely appalling, as both these border regions are in fact main mountain groups, rising to around 12,000 ft. To exacerbate the circumstances further, this was very much the transition period between winter and early spring. The high mountain passes and the mountains themselves to which the population escaped were still well covered in snow. The situation was to become even more complex, however, as towards the end of March and beginning of April considerable melting would take place, very quickly replacing the freezing conditions with an equally deadly emergency as temperatures rose, and clean water virtually disappeared.

Owing to political pressure, very much led by the media response to the emergency, Operation Safe Haven was set up, and military units from the United States, the United Kingdom, France, the Netherlands and a number of other countries were despatched to secure the region and begin humanitarian operations.

Date	Event
3 March 1991	Cease-fire agreed between Allied commanders and Iraqi counterparts. Shi'a uprising begins in southern Iraq
5	Revolt spreads as northern Kurds join uprising
7	Saddam Hussein orders Republican Guard to crush rebellions
10	US states its determination to stay out of 'Iraqi internal affairs'
19	Large areas of northern Iraq including oil city of Kirkuk under Kurdish control
30	Iraqi troops recapture Kirkuk
3 April	Iraqi troops recapture Kurdish city of Sulaymaniyah
7	Two million refugees reported fleeing from Iraqi army
9	John Major proposes UN-protected enclave for Kurds in northern Iraq
11	President Bush warns Iraq not to use air or ground forces in proposed safe enclaves: emergency aid to refugees stepped up
13	Cease-fire agreed between Kurdish guerrillas and Iraqi army
17	Bush and Major agree on need to police refugee camps
May	Main movement of Kurdish refugees down from mountains on Turkish border into protected enclave. Severe resettlement difficulties owing to earlier comprehensive destruction of village infrastructure
7–18	Inconclusive negotiations between Kurdish leaders and Baghdad on autonomy stalled by failure to obtain international guarantees on any deal
2 June	Kurds in border town of Zakho beg Allied forces to remain
15	British and US troops, as part of their phased withdrawal from Kurdish safe havens, prepare to hand over protection of Kurds to UN agencies and ill-equipped UN security guards
21	US temporarily halts withdrawal from northern Iraq following pressure from the European Community to allow more time to decide how best to ensure future security of Kurds
25	US announces plans to create a small allied rapid deployment force based in Turkey to protect the Kurds

Table 6 Kurdish uprising and Operation Safe Haven

My role in all of this was as Military Liaison Officer to the British Foreign Office Overseas Development Administration's (ODA) Response Team. After securing the area and making the temporary camps relatively safe, our main task was to begin Safe Haven 2, the process by which we would bring the people back down off the mountains to the relative comfort and safety of the plains.

Political/military communication

As I stated in my introduction, Safe Haven was carried out in two distinct phases. Phase One involved securing the area and bringing about the immediate relief of the displaced population – that was carried out in March/April 1991. Phase Two was the process of repatriation of the population back into Iraq from the Turkish border, and was carried out between May and July 1991.

Phase Two was hampered initially, I believe, by a serious lack of communication between government and the military on the ground, with particular regard to the true state of affairs in the region to which we were supposed to be returning the population.

Since the mid 1980s the Iraqi regime had been involved in carrying out a long term operation to displace the Kurdish population from its traditional villages. This operation, code named ANFAL, involved the mass deportation of populations either into guarded enclaves, or into the main urban areas. It also involved the mass slaughter of tens of thousands of people, specifically targeting the young male population. As part of the operation, the Iraqi regime had as an important aim the assured destruction of the villages together with the local agrarian infra-structure. To ensure the permanence of this process, efficient demolition was carried out by military engineers of key resources such as wells and pumping machinery, electrical plant and so on. Finally, a ghastly and efficient slaughter of farm animals was backed up by an extensive programme of defoliation and chemical poisoning. In the West we only saw a few public manifestations of this operation in the media – the most notorious being the gassing of more than 5000 inhabitants of the small border town of Halabja in March 1988.

So, when teams like ours set out to begin the repatriation phase, we had no idea whatsoever of what was ahead of us and what would have to be done to prepare the ground and make the villages and the land viable and capable of sustaining the returning population. We had not in any real sense been made party to the severity of the conditions that awaited us.

I am the first to accept that there are, and must be, genuine occasions when for reasons of national and international security, one has to be economic with strategic information. However, in this particular case, with the imminence of a major operational move of tens of thousands of refugees, unnecessary secrecy about what would turn out admittedly to be a set of embarrassing revelations of just how much our political masters had known about ANFAL and its dire consequences, considerably hampered the effectiveness of our operation and, I believe, significantly added to the suffering experienced by the returning population. It is one thing to be faced with the results of *ad hoc* and indiscriminate destruction of the sort one would expect from the event that happened in March 1991. It is of entirely another order altogether when you are faced with the reconstruction and rehabilitation necessary after a prolonged and sustained orgy of destruction as efficient as ANFAL.

We needed every advantage that could be afforded us in tackling these complexities.

Detailed information about the extent of destruction of the local infra-structure had been available at a higher level for some considerable time. However, the first information that the teams actually working on the ground received, which gave any indication whatsoever of the scale of destruction and therefore the scale and complexity of the task ahead of us, was the simple issue of up-to-date maps with the name of virtually every village in the region adjoined by the word 'destroyed' in purple.

In summing up, I would say that we were victims, at least initially, of what could only be described as an obsession with secrecy almost for its own sake. An important lesson that must be learned from this, when dealing with complex emergencies, is that agencies across the board have to pursue a degree of trust and information sharing to which hitherto they may not have been accustomed – especially governments.

Yes, the revelations were, and continue to be, embarrassing. That, however, is for politicians and future historians to sort out and apportion blame. Operationally, however, proverbial ostriches, with their heads stuck in the ground and hoping that these nasty people from the judiciary, the media and so on might go away and not notice, are a liability.

There cannot and should not be any place for the sort of institutionalised secrecy which often bedevils and inconveniences our day to day existence in situations like this where human lives can depend upon the speedy and, above all, honest transmission of key information, no matter how unpalatable, to those who need it. We needed to know, and nobody told us until too late.

I would like to move on now to another point where communication was not, especially in the beginning, at its best. This was communication between the military authorities on the ground and the United Nations High Commission for Refugees (UNHCR). To be fair to the UNHCR, a number of important lessons have been learned from this operation, lessons they managed to apply with some limited success in other theatres such as in Bosnia.

The UNHCR and the military authorities, especially those on the ground, only really started to come into daily contact with one another during Safe Haven 2. The UNHCR's own mandate, and therefore its preoccupation, was at that time purely with refugee repatriation. The problem here was that, once refugees were repatriated to their communities of origin, UNHCR generally felt itself discharged of further responsibility. However in the absence of a *sustainable* reintegration programme, repatriation of refugees can become a source of instability which in itself can lead to serious problems. The military authorities during this time were under considerable pressure to get the population off the mountains as quickly as possible. The pressure was twofold. Firstly, there was political pressure to get the people off the Turkish border and to make the area more secure. Quite frankly, nobody, ourselves or the Americans, wanted to be there in the first place. The second pressure was that there was anyway a real and genuine need to get these people off the mountains for humanitarian reasons. Their circumstances were becoming more and more untenable as each day passed.

Into this feverish activity entered the UNHCR, first of all in the person of a lady, whom I will call Miss Lim, who appeared at one of our co-ordination meetings and announced that during our process of repatriation, time, resources and effort would also have to be found to arrange for the registration of the returnees before we could repatriate them. Basically she would need tents, radios and military personnel to count and register each person as they came down. The effect of this announcement was, putting it mildly, devastating. We found it very difficult to imagine, and more importantly to justify, a process whereby tens of thousands of refugees in the most appalling conditions in some of the worst camps would simply march through tents, giving names, addresses and so on. We just could not understand the reasoning behind it. Even now, the names of camps like Cukurca and Kani Masi still conjure up images of hell-on-earth: stinking, fetid death traps where children died daily in their own filth.

UNHCR, who had their own good reasons for registration, did not let us in on the secret. The importance of families keeping in contact with each other, no matter what, was lost on us in our frenzied attempt to get these people off the mountains. There was no attempt whatsoever by UNHCR to engage military staffs in their reasoning; only a high handed insistence that 'this was how it was to be done'. Our mood was further soured by the subsequent appearance of a high ranking UNHCR official who, when we explained our misgivings, simply waved his hand and said 'Gentlemen, this is not Switzerland. These people – they are used to this sort of thing.' The slanging match that ensued afterwards led to misrepresentations in the press of the military trying to force repatriation on unwilling people at gun point and at the same time the military accusing the UNHCR of forcing people to wait up in the mountains against their will. Thus the opportunities for distrust and heightened tension were considerably multiplied. A simple misunderstanding of each group's roles, priorities and protocols, each valid and sensible for its own purposes, could have been overcome by careful dialogue and joint planning. It didn't happen.

Communication with Non-Governmental Organisations (NGOs)

In many ways the experience in northern Iraq was seminal with regard to communication between NGOs and the military, and a number of key lessons have been learnt and applied in other spheres such as Bosnia and Rwanda – sadly, however, not all. In discussions with representatives of major NGOs such as Save the Children Fund certain key factors were identified, both during and after the event. Here are some of them.

NGOs will naturally be suspicious of military intelligence gathering activities *per se*, and will especially be concerned that any association with them may compromise the NGOs' position of trust with both population and its donors, and may also lead, in their estimation, to unwanted problems of personal security for their staff. The key to overcoming this understandable problem was to be as up-front as possible. In this instance I believe the military and the NGOs scored quite well. Certainly, subsequent conversations that I have had with Save the Children Fund and other NGO personnel tend to bear this conclusion out. The very fact that people like myself were appointed as Military Liaison Officers to NGOs and volunteers, with a specific brief to be as open as possible, was in itself a major step in the right direction. To maintain this openness, whilst being careful not to breach and compromise genuine security considerations, was a considerable challenge to an organisation not best known for its enthusiasm for openness under operational conditions. This open communication proved generally of great benefit to both parties.

Another example of this was the formation of the Kurdish Liaison Team – a joint services team whose particular role was, whilst having as low a military profile as possible, to engage in what can best be described as friendly debriefing of the population. This unit's particular role was to gather the detailed information necessary for re-establishment of the local civil administration. However, they were also given a specific remit to pass on useful information to the NGOs – this seemed to work very well. On the American side, their Civil Affairs Teams again kept very regular contact and good communication with NGOs.

Another key element was the openness with which, obviously apart from purely security operations, the military made technical communications facilities open to NGOs, considerably enhancing the NGOs' own ability to communicate either with each other or with their own headquarters.

The lesson was certainly well learnt that in complex emergencies, where there must by necessity be a mixture of civilian and military personnel, great emphasis must be placed on the free transfer of information, together with sensible access to communications systems with a minimum of unnecessary bureaucracy.

Interestingly enough, in northern Iraq the military themselves also underwent a fairly steep learning curve in some of their own methods from contact with NGOs. Somewhere where contact and good communication with the NGOs really helped was in modifying quite radically some of the military's practices with respect to the provision of primary health care to the population. At the beginning the military tended to use their traditional field hospital type of set up. However, close co-operation with the NGOs showed that in fact what was needed was more specifically targeted basic hygiene care. This turned out to be an extensive and very rewarding joint effort, and after four to five weeks, this actually resulted in considerably reduced mortality, especially amongst children and infants. Indeed on the ground it significantly helped the morale of the soldiers, because it helped give them a feeling of usefulness, not only on the security side, but in actually being able to help refugees practically. All this could never have happened without this open contact between military and NGOs on the ground. It was very much a two-way thing, often resulting in quite fundamental modification of command and control structures. A real plus was that the military began regularly to take part in joint working groups at the Zakko headquarters, whence free and open exchange of information and views obtained.

When the thing didn't work, the negative results could be very telling. An example of this that comes to mind, particularly because of the harrowing human dimension, was a confrontation we had at a border camp called Cukurca.

One of my early tasks was to evaluate conditions in the camps, with a view to targeting military and ODA resources where they were most needed. As part of this, we flew into each camp by helicopter, to see conditions for ourselves and offer help where appropriate.

When we landed at Cukurca, we found the camp in complete chaos, with dysentery rife. It was obvious from the outset that the NGO was not coping – indeed they were overwhelmed. However, their response to our offer of assistance was to turn it down flat, saying categorically that they were able to cope without us. Not wishing to antagonise them we re-embarked, already committed to intervene, whether they liked it or not. However, as we were about to leave, a group of Kurdish doctors broke through and begged us not to believe what we had been told. This incident left a very bad taste in my mouth. Unfortunately, it was symptomatic of something that ran much deeper than simple NGO/military antagonisms.

Communication between NGOs

One thing which has been a matter of great interest to me in my current post at the Home Office Emergency Planning College is the number of people from the same local authority or the same area, in positions of responsibility for emergency planning of one sort or another, who had never met until they attended a course at the college. Of course there is pressure of work, and we all know about that and how it limits the time that we can give to things outside our own specific area of concern. It is all too easy to avoid the distractions of other people's problems. Nevertheless, genuine communication is too important to simply be a bolt-on function, because when the wheel really comes off, it is that personal contact and trust that can make a real difference in practice as to how an emergency is handled.

When I was working in northern Iraq evidence of the existence of this same problem appeared at almost every level amongst NGOs. This can at least partly be explained by differences in culture and organisational approach. More worrying though was the fact that there was also real evidence of some positive discouragement against information sharing and co-operation amongst NGOs in the field. It had to be assumed then that this was equally reflected much further up the chain. So, why should this be? The following thoughts may not be particularly complimentary to the emergency aid industry, but their basic reasoning is not advanced either lightly or in isolation. These views are generally held by a number of professionals in the field.

Nobody can doubt that the humanitarian NGOs represent a profound expression of human compassion. Nevertheless, the abrogation by governments of some of their responsibilities towards people *in extremis*, together with the pushing of these responsibilities at quite a high level onto NGOs, has, I believe, had a marked and deleterious effect on how aid is delivered. Quite frankly what seems to have occurred over the past few years is a growing culture of government sponsored competitive tendering by international NGOs for aid money. This competitive element has, without a doubt, tended to militate against the sort of information sharing that is crucial in complex emergency situations. In a number of cases this has encouraged the establishment of what can only be described as a culture of market-led aid.

This is especially exacerbated in the competition between the emerging small NGOs and the larger NGOs. I saw this on a number of occasions, especially amongst the small and local NGOs that were formed as a direct result of the emergency in northern Iraq. Indeed, small, largely unregulated NGOs proliferated wildly in the early days of the emergency. Operationally their effectiveness varied from the very good to the truly appalling. Regulation, there was virtually none; but that's another story. Later in this chapter I will explore some of these issues further, as they had a very direct effect on NGO relationships with the media, in what could almost be described as a situation of two-way manipulation.

As a direct consequence of all this, the military on a number of occasions found themselves in situations where they had almost to force some NGOs to sit down at the same table even just to talk to each other about sharing information and resources. Indeed in all honesty one got the sense that the simple pursuit of, and competition for, resources drove far too many of these institutions, at the expense of genuine co-operation. This is one situation I can only see getting worse. For with declining resources being made available for the less attention grabbing and vote winning development and preventive work, and correspondingly greater resources devoted to emergency aid, agencies are packaging programmes in order simply to capture humanitarian relief dollars. This will obviously make them very reluctant to communicate and co-operate with each other in sharing key information that may lose them the edge in the new *commercial* atmosphere. To say that I did find, and still find, the whole business unedifying would be to put it mildly.

Communication between all agencies and the local population

If you asked most practitioners who have actually worked on any type of emergency relief situation on the ground, they would almost take it as read, that one of the keys to accelerated recovery in any large scale emergency is to engage and use the skills and infra-structure of the affected population at the earliest possible opportunity. This not only decreases the actual physical burden on the relief agencies themselves, but, of equal importance, can have a profound effect on the morale of the affected population itself. They find themselves no longer merely part the problem, but active participants in the solution. Again it should be obvious that the only way that this can be achieved is if, at the very earliest opportunity, effective mechanisms for cross-communication between the responding agencies and the local population are put in place. This communication can start from simple grass roots exercises such as calling meetings, inviting local practitioners, doctors, engineers and local leaders to take part in the recovery planning process.

The great temptation in all of these situations, especially when you have got a number of agencies involved, is that even if these meetings are set up, they often become merely an opportunity for the agencies to issue their plans and get what they consider to be the appropriate response to their plans. I feel very strongly from my experience in northern Iraq that the key to success at this level is to do considerably less talking and more listening. This is often difficult to achieve, especially when relief agencies are under a great deal of pressure, whether by time or circumstances, to get on with the job. On the ground in northern Iraq there were some striking successes when the local population were allowed to be fully engaged in the relief effort. There was one well known marines officer who very quickly set up a local self-help committee in the town of Amadea and he gained great respect for his work.

However, at the strategic level, and as time wore on this became more and more apparent, there was, as indeed there still is, great reluctance to engage local communities fully in the recovery structure. Quite bluntly, even now communication with local institutions in the region is not good. I cite the example of the failure of the major agencies such as the UNHCR and UNICEF to have any meaningful communication and contact with the locally elected regional assembly that the people themselves set up in the town of Irbil to try and tackle the problems caused by the unilateral withdrawal by Baghdad of all its essential services and personnel. For complex political and other reasons this problem still has not been solved.

On a day-to-day level this lack of communication can result in misuse or misdirection of resources, funding and personnel, resulting in very high wastage rates. At its worst, as has happened in northern Iraq, failure to engage the local people and infra-structure, together with almost total dependence on linkages between major government and international organisations and NGOs, to the exclusion of local organisations, has resulted in complete breakdown of many local institutions. In the case of northern Iraq, this has contributed significantly to the next round of conflict and violence which is taking place in the region as I write.

Precisely the same communication breakdown occurred recently in Somalia, with ongoing results we know only too well (UNDHA 1995). It seems strange when we consider that one of the keys to the success of recovery programmes in the UK, such as those after the Towyn and Perthshire floods, has been this total involvement and engagement of the local population, at grass roots level.

Communication with the media

Running almost in parallel with each other have been the end of the cold war and an upsurge in what I would call resource wars, together with the complex emergencies that result from them.

Resource wars, often identified with ethnic loyalties, have created an explosion in political violence and human suffering. From 10 wars in 1959 there are at the moment now more than 50 being waged, whilst from less than 10 million refugees in 1980, the world now has at a conservative estimate about 23 million. In response to this a significant shift from development to emergency aid has occurred. From less than 200 million dollars in 1971 emergency aid spending by the OECD countries has expanded to somewhere around two and a half billion dollars. This is big business and the competition between the humanitarian NGOs and the human rights organisations is intense. The designer flags, tee-shirts, watches, flack jackets and other branded apparel of the new humanitarian workers jostling for television profiles testify to this. What we are actually seeing is a sort of market-led humanitarian industry. This isn't just my own opinion; in fact Oxfam recently came to broadly the same conclusions.

Taking all this a step further; markets are, in theory, regulated by consumer choice. However, in humanitarian emergencies, the *consumers* are usually destitute, and all too often excluded from planning and co-ordination meetings. If refugees and other disaster victims are unable to exercise a role in the planning of their own recovery, then this market driven humanitarianism is going to be mainly responsible to the other main category of consumer, that is, the major political donors and, frankly, local security forces, of whatever quality. What also happens is that the more tight-lipped but effective organisations on the ground such as the International Committee of the Red Cross (ICRC) become victims of this. For example, one process that happens all too frequently now is UN/NGO negotiated access programmes, such Lifeline Sudan and Operation Restore Hope in Somalia. None of these programmes involved local populations in deciding how they operated. More worrying is that these processes also confer legitimacy upon warring parties and facilitate the incorporation of relief aid into military strategies. This is now precisely the problem in northern Iraq. Given the media profile that NGOs more and more feel obliged to seek, it is rather obvious why insurgents prefer the international NGOs to the more publicity-shy and traditional international organisations such as the Red Cross. I would go even further, and say that, in pursuit of televised humanitarian success some Western politicians are now much less likely to finance organisations such as the Red Cross than the publicity hungry new humanitarian contractors. In fact, there is a deep paradox now that, with the rapid expansion of the humanitarian industry, there has been a simultaneous decline in refugee welfare and protection standards.

If, however, you want the upside of media intervention and co-operation between humanitarian NGOs, there are a number of noble examples. There is no doubt in my mind that Safe Haven, rather than being the creation of John Major, George Bush, the Turkish government or anyone else in that exalted company, was almost entirely the creation of the public odium invoked by the terrible images transmitted by the media. Who could say that that was wrong?

However, when it does go wrong, quite significant damage can be done to relief efforts. It is therefore critical that all relief agencies take a very responsible attitude towards accurate reporting of events over which they have some mandate or control, and where the media are found to be wanting, to make great efforts to correct them. It is not an exaggeration to say that one negative image can decimate a relief effort. Thankfully, not many occurred in our theatre of operations, but the ones that did occur had great potential for mischief.

Conclusions

One theme that I hope has carried itself throughout these few thoughts is that, accepting the fact that each complex emergency is unique, we must have the ability to fine tune our response to the needs of the affected population. Also, we must be capable of responding so as to maximise *their* ability to play a full and active role in their own recovery process. It has been shown time and time again (and I have witnessed the negative and the positive aspects of this in northern Iraq) that, unless we are prepared to listen as well as talk, the sustainability of any relief or recovery programme is put at risk.

It is of vital importance that all agencies, whether government or otherwise, address themselves to the questions of secrecy and confidentiality. We must have the intelligence, courage and generosity of spirit to accept that, in the extreme circumstances engendered by disasters and complex emergencies, there is no place for unnecessary and gratuitous subterfuge.

As we approach the close of the twentieth century, pessimists will tell us that the opportunities for disaster can only multiply. That may be the case and, if so, we shall all just have to learn to live with it, mitigating and planning as best we can.

However, one thing we certainly need not accept is poor and mismanaged communication – inter-personal or inter-agency. Technology has carried us far in our ability to exchange information and ideas. It is now up to us to take full advantage of the means at our disposal.

Reference

UNDHA (1995) *UNDHA News* issue 14

Acknowledgements

Terry Giles, Save the Children Fund
Ben Cornwall, Mines Advisory Group

8 CIVIL EMERGENCIES AND THE MEDIA: A CENTRAL GOVERNMENT PERSPECTIVE

Michael Granatt

This chapter addresses some of the issues and consequences which flow from the extraordinary attention which a disaster attracts. Successful handling of the aftermath of a disaster depends greatly on how well all the various communities of interest are kept informed and involved.

The aim of this chapter is to use some examples of experience and good practice to stimulate awareness and appropriate preparation. It gives an overview of some of the issues and practicalities of media handling and public information and provides some examples and some proven strategies. It also gives particular details of the role that central government and parliament will play.

For the sake of simplicity, the expression *disaster relief workers* is used to describe all those people helping the return to normality.

Disasters and news

Disasters contain the very essence of hard news.

They involve ordinary people, with whom everyone can identify, who have become the victims of extraordinary and horrible events. Few stories have such a powerful draw for the potential reader, listener and viewer – and therefore the media.

Intense media interest in a disaster is inevitable, and to many people it can seem almost as bad as the disaster itself. But dealing effectively with the media is an essential element of managing the aftermath. It is a major element of the public information process, serving the interests of the local community, disaster workers and the wider public interest.

Inadequate media and information handling worsens the problems of the aftermath. The biggest sufferer is the truth and those who rely on it, particularly victims.

Misleading, often hurtful, rumour can spread like wildfire. Inevitably, a response has to be made, lost ground has to be regained, and somebody has to organise it. Energy and resources are drained just when the load is heaviest.

Therefore media and public information handling must be built into emergency planning and training. It is essential to involve those at the highest levels. On the day, they will be involved – as decision makers, leaders and participants.

Good media and public information handling can deliver these objectives:

- sympathetic coverage for the victims, generating support from opinion formers and the wider community

- positive coverage of the work of disaster relief workers, reinforcing morale, and developing public understanding of their difficulties

- public confidence in the handling of the aftermath

- a fund of goodwill among the media for help with publicity, or for restraint

- the moral high ground from which to deal with misbehaviour.

Victims

Public attitudes to disaster coverage are ambivalent. Many people who condemn the 'intrusion' clearly continue to buy the intruder's products. A notable exception is the London *Sun*, still suffering a boycott by Merseysiders outraged by unsubstantiated reports which blamed Liverpool supporters for the Hillsborough disaster.

Research conducted for the United Kingdom Broadcasting Standards Council by Anne Shearer (1991) has confirmed that many disaster victims have no great concern over normal media attention. It is also wrong to assume they will all wish to be kept away from reporters. Some may never wish to see a journalist or a camera again, but others will welcome the opportunity to share the burden of their experiences.

Relatives may well hear the initial report through the media without realising it is directly relevant to them. While personal news should reach them first through official channels, there are many instances where a news flash or a reporter's call has been the first news of a loved one's involvement.

On 26 February 1993 a bomb exploded in a car park above an underground railway station at the foot of New York's World Trade Center. The building comprises twin 110-storey towers, the workplace of more than 40,000 people. Five died, 1000 were injured, and smoke poured up through the towers.

Many people had to walk down many dozens of flights of stairs. Some went to the roof to wait for helicopters. Others stayed put, and sought information from television and radio. Some of the local broadcasters invited those who were trapped to phone in, and then broadcast conversations with them live into programmes. It was not smooth running. The *Sunday Times* (1993) reported:

'A major role was played by television and radio stations. Workers trapped on upper floors called in and newscasters gave advice liberally and sometimes dangerously. Millions of viewers saw the raw drama unfold. Isaiha Rivera, a technician, called one station from the 110th floor and pleaded: 'What do we do? Walk or stay?' John Cure, a money broker on the 51st floor, asked Channel Nine's Frank Field how he could get help as all the 911 emergency lines jammed. Field told people to smash windows, until fire officers [on the ground outside the building] complained that they were being showered with broken glass.'

On the same day, bombs planted by terrorists exploded at a British Gas storage site in Warrington, Cheshire. It was in the early morning, and as a result there were fires and a large explosion. Fortunately, very considerable damage to homes and injury were avoided but 200 families had to be evacuated and there was considerable disruption to traffic on nearby main roads.

Local radio reporters interviewed police, local authority and fire service officials and reported from the scene. The radio station handled traffic reports and officials' reassurances about the progress of the operation to tackle the fire. It fed much of this information to national radio and television. In short, apart from the news operation, the local radio station was heavily and willingly involved in providing public service information and rumour control.

Exhibit 1 The unexpected adviser

After the first contact, most will glean all they can from broadcasts and newspapers. They may well come to regard those sources as more credible than officials whom they may come to regard as obstructive or unhelpful, or party to some cover-up. When formalities appear to be blocking news or even the return of their relatives' effects, the media will provide information and often champion their cause. A relative of a victim of the Lockerbie disaster has described the media has as 'our greatest ally in the fight for the victims of Pan Am 103'.

The role of the media

Most people first hear of a disaster through the media. Indeed, most of what they ever learn about it will probably come through television, radio or newspapers. To a considerable degree, the same is true for those directly affected, whether it is a town or a village, or just a group of people with a common interest.

The reasons are simple. As information processors, the media are better resourced, faster, less constrained and more accessible than anybody else involved. Their business is the unusual. Their techniques and technology are designed to deal with crises.

Beyond the immediate aftermath, news coverage becomes a fascination, a mirror in which the community looks to see itself as others see it. The effect of news coverage on morale cannot be overstated. It makes effective media liaison a vital consideration for community leaders, disaster managers, and the managers of individual organisations.

Most disaster relief workers will be in the same position as the general public. Their personal interest in news reports will become intense, and their parent organisations will not have the resources (or even the overview) to compete. Emergency workers are often reluctant to take their woes home, so their families and friends will often only be able to understand their difficulties from news reports.

Opinion formers – people whose comments influence the community, the government, local authorities, private companies or any other group – also get their vital first impressions from the media. So do markets.

Of course, the media do not comprise a single organisation or have a single purpose. They have different audiences and different concerns. For the local community, including relief workers, local media play a critical role. Their audience sees them as part of the community, sources of information and advice, as well as news.

Communities and individuals can be hurt by *lack* of media attention. Many will feel deeply that this demonstrates a general lack of interest in their plight.

They are right. Fair or not, the importance of any event is measured by public and politicians according to the level of media attention. Seeing *is* believing.

The Towyn flood disaster in Wales made 5000 people homeless. Many were angry that the national media lost interest. They wanted the public and governmental support which is stimulated by extensive news coverage.

The same happened in France after the 1987 hurricane that hit Brittany and south east England. With no media coverage, the result was a 'national deficit of attention', according to a legislative representative from the area.

The victims of London's *Marchioness* riverboat disaster discovered a dark side of ill-informed coverage. Public sympathy was dimmed by implications that they were 'just' rich yuppies. In fact they were ordinary young people at a party.

The problem arose because the only information available to the media was second-hand and speculative. The reporting process – particularly broadcasting – uses interviews with survivors or relatives to characterise the people involved. But the media had little chance to describe the partygoers accurately. The survivors had been dispersed to a number of hospitals and some had simply gone home. So all the descriptions available came from secondary sources such as riverboat workers whose impressions were hazy and opinionated.

The frustration and anger of the survivors and the relatives of the dead is still evident. No-one knows how much grief would have been averted by better informed public opinion at the time. The job of the journalist – and it is a task. in which they should be helped – is accurately to report the human tragedy. Without that essential ingredient, public reaction will focus on mangled metal rather than mangled lives.

Exhibit 2 Out of sight, out of mind

The local media will be there long after the nationals have vanished, informing and often supporting local people. They also have the important ability to deal authoritatively with rumours or with partial information carried by the national media. The role of the local media is explored more fully in Chapters 5 and 6.

The immediate aftermath gives local radio a special role, because great numbers of people at home and in vehicles will immediately tune in. After a disaster, a very high priority must be given to providing local radio with frequent, accurate, and timely information.

Local newspapers lack the immediacy of broadcasting, but they can provide much more detail and advice in a form which can be kept, referred to and passed on. Local newspapers must be kept well briefed.

In essence: as the media spread the news, they move hearts, minds and morale. They influence the flow of sympathy and support: financial, physical, psychological and political.

The media process

Disasters make enormous demands on everybody – including the media. There has always been great pressure for information and pictures, but increasing competition and the growing number of outlets has magnified the problem enormously.

The three Ms

But whatever the disaster, and whatever its size, the pattern of media enquiries and subsequent reporting always falls into these recognisable phases:

- **Mayhem:** the immediate aftermath: a mad scramble to know what, where, when, why and how, and to get the picture
- **Mastermind:** a search for all the relevant background information and history
- **Manhunt:** the search for error, fault, and the head that must roll
- **The Epilogue:** the long-term aftermath and follow-up; the inquiries, trials, memorial services, reconstructions and documentaries.

The three Ms manifest themselves very quickly. The cycle took nearly 20 hours in the coverage of Piper Alpha but three hours in the Clapham Junction rail crash. The Epilogue can last for years.

Phone bashing is the telephonic equivalent of the physical rush to the scene. As news comes in, news room reporters ring all likely official and informal sources. They comb local telephone directories, seeking witnesses willing to talk or even be interviewed for broadcast news bulletins. They ring every government department local council, emergency service and hospital likely to be involved.

Expert comment is sought, both for guidance in following the story, and for quotation. Most major news organisations keep lists of experts who are often retained to be available for instant quotation at any time. 'I'm not an expert on anything except how to become an instant expert' said a reporter on a major national newspaper, describing his experience of Lockerbie. 'We had our expert on call, and I knew how to get the information out of his head and into my copy.'

He was working on just one of the dozens of major news rooms involved within minutes of the disaster. His news editor put 12 reporters on the phones at the same time as he was dispatching another dozen to Scotland.

Some news room reporters will comb databases for background material while other staff read incoming copy from news agencies and keep a close eye on the competition.

And if the story is big enough, the television and radio news chiefs negotiate extra bulletin time with network control. That is an increasing likelihood because of the competitive pressure from 24-hour news stations.

For the biggest incidents they bid to take over the network entirely, an arrangement known as Operation Openender by ITN and the independent television companies. The consequence is an enormous increase in the pressure on news staff for material – pressure they in turn put on all their sources.

Exhibit 3 Bashing the phones

The thirst for pictures often seems exaggerated. Even though 'quality' newspapers depend on the gathering, analysis and presentation of information, every newspaper requires striking, high-quality photographs.

All media also need a staple diet of good, timely information. A gentle flow punctuated by set-piece press conferences is the best routine. For newspapers and radio, this is a major part of their diet.

Television has special needs. It can only operate effectively for its audience – the biggest and most easily influenced – if it has relevant, meaningful, up-to-the-minute pictures. Its technology and demands can make it the most intrusive medium, but it also has very considerable power to set the agenda.

As broadcasting crews and newspaper staff are dispatched to the scene, their headquarters news rooms will be just as busy. Reporters will be 'bashing' the phones and editors will be watching the competition like hawks.

Much the same will be happening in newspaper offices. Newspapers also compete using pictures (which they can receive equally quickly), but their primary objectives will be detail and description. Two pages of a broadsheet newspaper can carry easily more information than a 25-minute television bulletin.

Some photographers and reporters act outrageously. The remedies are to leave little vacuum for them to fill and thereby little excuse for their actions; to develop general awareness of their presence; and to condemn them openly and quickly. It is also essential to complain to their editors. Beware, however, of exacerbating the distress of victims.

Accuracy and clarity are vital in dealing with the media. All official information must be checked before release. Media output should be monitored and inaccuracy dealt with immediately and at subsequent press conferences.

There must be a constant dialogue with the media to deal with inaccurate information before it takes root. The media should be able to reach official sources at any time to check stories. If official sources cannot provide good information swiftly, the media will go elsewhere with obvious consequences; those with the information will have only themselves to blame.

It is always better to provide facilities for the media than to live under the illusion that they are a problem which will go away. News-gatherers must do their jobs one way or another, and it is better to use the process constructively than be a victim of it. At the end of this chapter is a check list which can help meet this aim.

Media handlers

Constructive attitudes among media handlers are essential. In the midst of chaos, when tempers are fraying and stress is high, the simple presence of cameras and notebooks is provocative. Journalists are often an easy and obvious target for the release of frustrations. A primary task of the media handler must be to minimise friction.

A poor attitude is very dangerous. Bloody-mindedness is infectious and revenge is sweet. Condescension is infuriating and angry people are neither receptive nor co-operative. Frankness, openness, professionalism, courtesy and understanding are powerful advocates. They are the essential tools of the media handler.

There is no magic formula. Media handling requires people who can negotiate sensible arrangements. When you look for candidates, seek people

- with some relevant experience,
- who have had or will absorb some training
- who display negotiating and leadership skills
- who have great reserves of patience and good humour
- who possess, above all, a truck-load of common sense.

They must be team players, willing and able to liaise effectively with all their counterparts. Accuracy, sensitivity, urgency, co-ordination and co-operation are key operational watchwords.

Management matters

Despite the great tide of news coverage, outside help and other activity which engulfs a community after a disaster, many of those involved still feel isolated and badly informed. They want, and need, to be kept informed and to be told that the world cares.

This is instinctively understood in the case of victims or their relatives. However, it is just as important for relief workers, especially if the aftermath is prolonged.

There will be people who are coping with the unthinkable in hospitals and mortuaries; others who will be providing meals hour after hour from inadequate kitchens; yet others who are shouldering the emotional problems of shocked survivors. They will all be watching the media, as will their families and the whole affected community. People will work their hearts out to help in a crisis, but nothing can damage their morale more quickly than a belief that their efforts are unappreciated.

All of them will deserve and need praise and support, both in public and in private. In many ways, therefore, handling the media aspects of a disaster is a vital leadership role. There is nothing wrong in expressing pride in a job well done; indeed, it is very important to do just that.

At Lockerbie, one well-known voluntary group featured in news coverage, because of its parent body's traditional role and uniform. Local authority workers – doing the same job of feeding people – were not mentioned and suffered real loss of morale.

Information flow is the key, and it can generally be achieved in two ways.

First, direct methods. During the Chichester floods in February 1994, the Chief Fire Officer arranged for everyone involved in protecting the town centre to have a radio on his brigade's general net. Even the fitter from the county highways department, whose only (but vital) job was to tend a pump, was able to stay in touch with the whole operation. Over the days and then weeks of the emergency, this made a significant contribution to morale.

Another direct method is to ensure that the public affairs department provides copies of press notices to notice boards in canteens, rest rooms and so on, and to those holding team briefings. In their team meetings, managers should also convey the wider picture.

Second, indirect methods via the media. Make sure the messages being conveyed to the media include words for or about the relief workers. VIP press conferences can be particularly useful in this respect. Use internal systems to tell people when the chief executive is likely to appear on television. Circulate a digest of what he/she said via bulletin boards, notice boards or other systems.

Parliament and government

In the immediate aftermath of a major disaster in the UK, one government department will take the lead role (see Chapter 4). Often that process will be swift and obvious. For example, a civil aircraft crash will automatically involve the Department of Transport. In more complex circumstances, the Cabinet Office's Civil Contingency Unit will nominate the lead department.

Parliament expects the government to bring it the facts about any major civil emergency as soon as possible. For that reason, expect the lead department to get in touch with the lead agencies very early on. It might happen directly, or through the government regional offices. The ways in which central government may become involved are shown in Exhibit 4.

Official level contact

- telephone calls or visit by officials from the lead department or the government regional office for ministers' and parliament's information; or to assess need and/or offer help; or to reconnoitre a ministerial or a royal visit

- officials join the disaster management team to co-ordinate advice and support from units such as the Marine Pollution Control Unit, and from regulators or inspectors such as the Health and Safety Executive, National Rivers Authority, Ministry of Agriculture or Air Accident Investigation Branch of the Department of Transport. They may be following routine procedures and/or paving the way for more formal and exceptional enquiries.

Ministerial involvement may include

- telephone calls to cut through information barriers, to assess needs, to offer support and help, to lay the groundwork for a visit or parliamentary statement

- fact-finding visits to demonstrate government's concern and involvement, to facilitate support and help, to gather information for parliament and ministerial colleagues, to inform decision-making on, for example, the form of any inquiry.

Exhibit 4 Government contact

Within hours of a major site-specific disaster, a minister from the lead department will visit the scene. With the minister will be a private secretary, a press officer, and one or more officials from the relevant division. However, a visit to a wide-area disaster, for example, a flood, may not take place for a day or two. While they will keep closely in touch, ministers will not want to get under the feet of people during the immediate aftermath. Nor will they want to be perceived to be exploiting a disaster. For example, a minister will generally resist any media presence during hospital visits.

The minister will normally give an oral statement to the House of Commons at the first opportunity.

The minister will then answer questions for perhaps 30 minutes or more, a session which will be opened by the respective opposition front bench spokesman, followed by local MPs, and then other back benchers.

A typical parliamentary statement on a disaster includes

- a full description of the incident
- casualty information
- the response of the emergency services and other agencies
- the response of the government
- consequential action, including police inquiries, the setting up of a public inquiry
- expressions of sympathy and thanks.

The first reaction will be from the opposition front bench, the next from the local MP. These and other responses express views, but are also framed as questions to which the minister responds. The whole statement will be broadcast live on television and radio, and edited highlights will be used in news broadcasts. Ministers and opposition spokesmen may also be interviewed by the media afterwards.

The statement and the briefing for answers will be drawn up by lead department officials who will need comprehensive, accurate and fresh information. They will get this through their own officials on the scene, or by telephone. In either event, a nominated contact should channel enquiries and information, and should also respond to opposition spokesmen and local MPs. The nominated contact should keep closely in touch with all the press officers from the organisations directly involved, particularly the central government press officer who will take the lead in making media arrangements for the minister.

Exhibit 5 With permission Madam Speaker...

Above all, a minister will want to get a grasp of the situation and to ensure that central government is providing all the help it can. In particular, he or she will be acutely aware of the lead department's role in co-ordinating the government's response.

The minister will have been briefed by officials before arriving, and will be anxious to hear the views of those managing the aftermath. At the scene, the minister will wish to meet disaster workers, survivors, relatives, and members of the public to ensure that what is being done is appropriate, effective and swift. And the minister will want to do all of this before meeting the media for a news conference or interviews.

Ministers will normally report to Parliament through an oral statement to the House of Commons at the first opportunity after the event. How this is done is explained more fully in Exhibit 5.

Handling check list

This check list is necessarily generalised. Smaller incidents may not need all the elements described; very big incidents will need more.

1. At the site(s), organise media facilities (rendezvous points and vantage points) which ensure that rescue and other work continues unhindered, while allowing media personnel to do their jobs with a minimum of hindrance. Make use of established press card systems to exclude fools and ghouls, and ask the media to nominate pools to cover restricted facilities.

2. Put up spokespeople who are as senior as possible, clearly identifiable as such and who have been trained.

3. Establish a dialogue with the media, not only to discover their needs and requests, but to provide the means for dealing with problems and the dissemination of public information. That will require a focus: first, the rendezvous point mentioned above, and then some form of press centre which must be staffed as long as necessary, probably 24 hours a day.

4. Establish a flow of credible information. Set up a media co-ordinating group to mirror any overall control group and to oversee the press centre. Information for the media must be accurate, swift, authoritative, and consistent. It must be underwritten by all those involved, who should ideally speak with one voice. The co-ordinating group should log and record all information which is released, and ensure that all information providers (for example, HQ press officers) are kept up to date. The media must be able to check stories with official sources at any time.

5. A media strategy with clear objectives must be agreed by the disaster's control group, who must also review progress regularly.

The necessary specialist skills and advice must be represented there by the chairman of the media co-ordinating group, who will probably be the senior PR professional from the lead organisation.

6. The co-ordinating group should continually brief key staff at all levels on what the media are asking and saying. Media monitoring must be used to determine the effectiveness of the media strategy and to tackle misinformation.

7. Where organisations cannot take the same line, for example, where a regulatory body must speak independently, use the co-ordinating group to ensure that all those involved have a clear understanding of what is to be said before release.

8. Establish a collection plan for interesting, non-controversial information, which can fill the gaps between the releases of hard information about the event. Stories of individual endeavour, swift thinking, initiative, hardship, or selflessness, will always be available, and will play a valuable role in maintaining the focus of the media on official sources. (Some ways in which this was done following the Hillsborough disaster can be found in Chapter 11.)

9. Deal with poor media behaviour swiftly and directly, not only with the journalist concerned but also with the most senior editorial executive who can be contacted. Strong views may also be offered openly at press conferences, but beware of exacerbating the distress of victims, and make sure the facts are right.

10. Arrangements for VIP visits should be considered at an early stage, so that the inevitable disruption is kept to a minimum, and the benefits are maximised. There should be a nominated person to deal with these visits. VIP briefing must aim to ensure that the VIP who will talk has plenty of information from which to brief the media and others on the efforts and needs of all involved.

11. The complex needs of victims with respect to the media should be considered by the control group. Many walking and willing wounded may benefit by describing their experiences, while they shield those who want privacy.

12. Remind everybody that the man or woman with the notebook, or tape recorder, or camera, is trying to do their job, just as others

are. Unless they prove otherwise, they deserve the same courtesy and consideration as anybody else. Give none, and you will get none, despite all the smooth talking, elegant press releases, or robust responses you can muster

Finally, you will find in Exhibit 6 some of the questions to which the media wanted answers in the immediate aftermath of two disasters: the *Marchioness* riverboat sinking and the Piper Alpha oil platform accident. These may give you an inkling into the kind of preparation you need to make for dealing with the media when disaster strikes.

The Marchioness disaster on the River Thames on 21 August 1989 gave rise to thousands of calls in the first 24 hours, many from abroad. Press conferences held at New Scotland Yard involved a number of foreign TV crews, including some with no English. The information sought included

- from whom the first emergency calls came
- which emergency services got there first
- how many rescuers and rescue vessels were involved
- how they heard and from whom
- how many times they had done this before
- details of their training
- requests for facilities on rescue vessels
- numbers of passengers/dead/survivors, (for which there were no simple answers for some time)
- when and where the inquests would be held
- whether American victims' families would be better off suing in the USA
- complex legal questions on statutory requirements, rights of way on the river and the powers of the police to arrest people
- powers of the various regulatory authorities involved
- history of pleasure craft on the river

and many others.

Hundreds of media personnel and the public gathered on the banks of the river to watch the boat being raised. Survivors were interviewed, sometimes to the point of harassment. Unfounded rumour ran rife about a 'gay party' on board and the dangers of Aids and hepatitis to rescuers.

The media were particularly unhappy about being denied access to the best vantage point, Southwark Bridge, seemingly for reasons of taste, rather than for any operational purpose. Ironically, throughout the night television crews on the bridge had used their powerful lights to help the rescuers.

The Piper Alpha disaster in the North Sea on 6 July 1988 also generated thousands of telephone inquiries. A huge number of questions arose. They included

- numbers and nationalities of people on board; dead/survivors
- numbers and nationalities of rescue vessels
- chronology of the accident
- interview requests for inspectors, survivors, ministers, company officials, pilots, coastguards
- history of the platform, the North Sea and related disasters
- likely economic effects
- facility requests for other platforms and safety inspection visits
- technical background to North Sea activities
- every conceivable detail of the regulatory regimes
- comparisons of different platform types and of Norwegian and UK safety regimes
- detailed statistical information
- names of recent inspectors
- details of judicial and investigative procedures in the UK and USA
- insurance arrangements and liability of all the parties concerned
- industrial relations arrangements, rights and procedures
- comparison of rights of workers onshore and offshore
- regulations concerning smoking and drinking offshore
- safety equipment types, capacities, age, design and country of manufacture
- safety training regimes, arrangements and plans for the North Sea and the testing of those plans
- history of safety enforcement and the penalties for non-compliance
- how to put out oil fires
- how to spell Red Adair and the likely size of his bank balance
- analysis of licence holders and investors in the North Sea
- manufacturers and designers of all equipment on the platform
- which other platforms used the same equipment

- likely public inquiry and its remit, chairman, type, location, powers, witnesses and probable duration
- legal status, powers of and precedents for a disaster fund
- likely government, charitable or other donations to such a fund
- likely trustees
- history of disaster funds and common problems
- consultative arrangements with trades unions, companies and consultants
- history of trades union organisation offshore
- history of trades union complaints about safety problems.

Many local boats were chartered to take television crews out to the area of the platform. Aircraft were hired to get aerial shots. Hospitals were door-stepped to get pictures and interviews.

The first reporter contacted the Department of Energy at 22.10, just 12 minutes after the initial mayday call, and about 15 minutes before the final explosion which destroyed the platform.

Exhibit 6 Two disasters – hundreds of questions

References

Home Office (1997) *Dealing with Disaster* 3rd edition Liverpool: Brodie
Shearer, A. (1991) *Survivors and the Media* London: John Libbey
Sunday Times (1993) London: 28 February

PART III

THE HILLSBOROUGH DISASTER

THE HILLSBOROUGH DISASTER

This part of the book looks at one disaster: a crowd-related disaster at the Hillsborough football stadium. But the way in which the Hillsborough disaster unfolded, how it was reported and what happened afterwards teaches us lessons not about football grounds or football fans and how they should be managed. As we will see, the Hillsborough disaster has a great deal to tell us about the role of the media, about planning, organisation and management, and about caring for the victims.

There have been many crowd-related disasters, characterised by numbers of people being pushed, crushed or stampeding, resulting in injury and death. Such disasters have occurred in places as diverse as underground stations, dance halls, leisure centres and sporting venues. They have come about as a result of people hurrying to get into somewhere – or to get out. They have happened on stairs, on ramps, in tunnels and in doorways.

Anyone who has been in a confined space, with a restless group of people anxious to get on the next train or to avoid missing the start of a concert, may have been pushed and shoved, but suffered only from a sharp elbow in the ribs. Anyone who has been responsible for a place where people congregate – shop or factory, school or cinema, city fireworks display or village carnival – may have had to take decisions about directing members of the public so as to ensure their safety, and got it right.

This is the story of an event which went seriously, disastrously, fatally wrong.

On Saturday 15 April 1989, football fans began to arrive in Sheffield and head towards Hillsborough, the home ground of Sheffield Wednesday Football Club. They were supporters of Nottingham Forest and Liverpool, the two teams playing in the FA Cup semi-final at the neutral Hillsborough ground. Liverpool supporters were directed to the north and west ends of the ground, and as kick-off time approached a very large crowd of fans gathered there, at the Leppings Lane end. Clearly, they were not all going to get into the ground before 3 p.m.

In an attempt to prevent the fans outside the ground being crushed, the senior police officer arranged for one of the large exit gates to be opened, thus allowing an influx of fans on to the concourse area between the turnstiles and the back of the terraces. In front of the fans was an opening which led down to the penned terraces behind the goal. These central pens were, unknown to the supporters, already overcrowded, although the pens on either side were relatively empty. Fans walked straight on into the tunnel ahead of them, without knowing how crowded it was in front of them. As more and more people entered the tunnel, with no way of knowing what was happening in front, the crush began. Fans were crushed in the tunnel leading to the pens on the terrace and in the pens themselves as they were squeezed against perimeter fencing which had been erected to prevent pitch invasions. Ninety-five people died and many hundreds suffered serious injury.

The people who died at Hillsborough did not stampede or panic. A crazed stranger did not shoot them down. They did not die because a train hit the buffers or a ferry sailed with its bow doors open. They were ordinary football fans, going to cheer on their team, crushed by fellow supporters who were absolutely powerless to prevent their deaths.

While Part II of this book explained how a number of different crises and disasters were or would be dealt with by the communication professionals involved, in this part of the book we look at this one event, but from four perspectives. Each of the four authors gives his or her own account of what was happening, whether in the news room of the local paper in Liverpool, at an emotionally charged and smoke-filled drop-in centre, at a packed press conference in Sheffield's town hall or in the solemn atmosphere of the coroner's inquest. The four authors did not know each other before the Hillsborough disaster, they all worked in different jobs for different organisations, and they had nothing much in common professionally. On that sunny spring Saturday, each one was off duty. But by the evening they had all been plunged into a tragic disaster and they were at work.

Alf Green was, at the time of the Hillsborough disaster, the news editor of the Liverpool *Echo*. He had been in regional newspapers all his working life and had covered the Aberfan disaster referred to by

Peter Young in Chapter 1 of this book, as well as the Heysel stadium disaster, when Liverpool Football Club supporters were involved in another crowd-related disaster. His immediate response on the day of the Hillsborough disaster was that of the newspaper professional: to get the story and print it.

The contribution made by Alf Green is firmly from the point of view of the regional newspaper on Merseyside. His paper, the *Echo*, took the stance of sticking up for Merseyside and for those who had been bereaved, injured or simply outraged by the events at Hillsborough. He gives some striking examples in the form of headlines and page one leads, contrasting the *Echo*'s coverage with that of some of the national newspapers. Here is no dispassionate reporting of two sides of an argument, but a clear and utterly partisan approach. In more recent years the idea that the journalists can and should take sides has begun to gain currency. But when Alf Green's front pages hit the streets this was uncommon.

Paddy Marley was a lifelong council worker. He had started with Liverpool Council as a school leaver more than thirty years previously and worked his way through the ranks, mostly in the field of personnel and industrial relations. He reached his job as assistant director (administration) in the social services department in 1985. He was not a social worker – indeed he stands shoulder to shoulder with many ordinary Merseysiders in claiming he would not knowingly invite a 'busybody' social worker into his house – but an organiser: his immediate response was to get things done for the victims and their relatives. His involvement and that of his team was many-faceted.

In addition to dealing with the immediate needs of victims, such as cash for food, suitable mourning clothes and funeral expenses, he set up a number of initiatives, including a helpline, drop-in centres and a newsletter for victims and their supporters. He gives a vivid account of the turmoil into which his department was thrown, with so many demands on it and no previous experience to draw upon. When his work on the aftermath of the disaster was accomplished he locked himself in his office for two weeks and completely re-wrote the council's emergency plan, to take account of what had happened.

Peter Hayes, who is now retired, had been a police officer for 32 years at the time of the Hillsborough disaster. He was the Deputy Chief Constable of the South Yorkshire Police, a force which had recently been in the public eye because of its handling of the miners' strike. His first response was to get to work and look after his staff.

South Yorkshire Police's involvement in the Hillsborough disaster was not simply that of the local force policing a football match. They were, as always, responsible for ensuring that public order was maintained on their patch. But their responsibility for Hillsborough was very much greater. It was clear from the outset that a police officer had authorised the opening of a gate to let in a large number of fans, who were in danger of serious injury outside the stadium. This resulted in the disaster inside the ground. Because of the organisational failure in crowd control which caused the Hillsborough disaster, South Yorkshire Police became the focus of another disaster – their own.

Chapter 12 tells the story of the crisis which hit the South Yorkshire Police force, and how they coped with it. So when Peter Hayes refers to crisis management in this context, he is not referring to an organisation's response to an external event such as a major disaster, but rather to that sort of crisis which can occur within an organisation when, as a result of an event – internal or external – its normal functions are so disrupted, the confusion and turbulence so great, that the steady-state of the organisation itself is seriously interrupted.

I was the chief publicity officer for Sheffield Council when the Hillsborough disaster happened. Sheffield was one of the first local authorities to employ a publicity officer in the 1970s and by 1986 he had retired, leaving a department of over 30 staff. He was replaced by me – a woman thirty years his junior, with no previous local authority experience. I had reorganised the staff into teams, including a press team who had established themselves as the first point of contact for the media. The council's plan for peacetime emergencies gave my home telephone number, and that was about it. My first response was to find out what was happening and respond on behalf of the council.

Until the final verdict of the coroner's court almost two years after the disaster itself, it was uncertain whether Sheffield Council would be found to have borne some responsibility for the tragedy. Throughout that period there were many hundreds of journalists from Britain and overseas in the city and in the town hall (where most of the newsworthy action took place) and Chapter 11 describes how the press team tried to keep them satisfied.

Each of the chapters which follows gives an account of the immediate response, the immediate aftermath, and the longer-term implications of what happened and how it was dealt with. Each author tries to draw some conclusions and provide pointers to good practice. There is some repetition, and some inconsistency in what is written. This is not the result of sloppy editing. It is the result of a deliberate decision to allow each author to tell his or her own story, as they saw it. The Hillsborough disaster and the way in which it was investigated and reported caused immense controversy and polarisation of opinion. It is to be hoped that the reader will look at the disaster from these four viewpoints and thus see the full picture with greater clarity.

There is one vital lesson which comes from all the contributors to this part of the book. Although there had been many crowd-related disasters before, and the build-up to Hillsborough was gradual, the disaster simply happened, one April afternoon, and those caught up in it were more or less unprepared for what hit them.

In telling the story of Hillsborough from their respective viewpoints, the authors hope you will be able to benefit from their hindsight.

9   A NEWSPAPER AT THE HEART OF THE HILLSBOROUGH TRAGEDY

Alf Green MBE

It was a beautiful afternoon and an idyllic setting. Spring was reflected everywhere as the sunlight bounced off the waters of the Dee. The linear park along the Wirral bank of the river was a haven of tranquillity. I fiddled with the tuning button on my tiny portable radio to find the local station. Suddenly it was there – right in my ear. 'The game at Hillsborough has been stopped. People are spilling on to the pitch behind the Liverpool goal ... '.

Those two terse sentences signalled, for me, the end of a peaceful family afternoon, and the start of a heart-breaking tragedy, a tragedy which shocked the nation and stunned the city of Liverpool.

The name Hillsborough and the date, 15 April 1989, are burned into the memories of the people of Liverpool and the greater area of Merseyside. They found themselves at the centre of the worst disaster in British sporting history. Ninety-five people died at the scene, four hundred were seriously hurt and thousands were psychologically scarred, some for life.

During the week that followed, the people of Merseyside were subjected to intense media activity on a global scale. The behaviour of a few journalists, and several newspapers, did little to enhance the reputation of sections of the national press. The way in which some reports were angled to blame the disaster on drunken football yobs, dressed of course in Liverpool shirts, created a myth that has come back to haunt the bereaved and survivors on several occasions.

Time has not yet healed the hurt of Hillsborough. It is a disaster that refuses to be forgotten. Those touched by it continue to fight for the justice they firmly believe has been denied to them – despite a Home Office inquiry, a massive police investigation, an inquest, and a whole series of out of court financial settlements.

The final report of the Hillsborough Project was published in November 1995 – a six year study commissioned by Liverpool City Council (Scraton et al. 1995). It provides a detailed and critical analysis of the aftermath of Hillsborough, examining the way in which evidence was put before the public inquiry and inquests, and the extensive media coverage these attracted. Its title *No Last Rights* and sub-title *The Denial of Justice and the Promotion of Myth in the Aftermath of the Hillsborough Disaster* reflect the views expressed by Professor Phil Scraton and co-authors Ann Jemphrey and Sheila Coleman, of Edge Hill University College, Ormskirk. They are critical of the way in which many national papers linked Hillsborough with Heysel, the Belgian soccer disaster four years earlier in which the riotous behaviour of some Liverpool fans contributed to the death of 39 Juventus supporters. They also point to the prominence given to allegations of drunkenness, especially those made by police officers, with little space and prominence being given to contrary statements.

Hillsborough was an exceptional disaster in a number of ways.

- It was a disaster which occurred in one city and left another city, 50 miles away, wracked with grief.

- Horrific scenes on the terraces unfolded before a live audience of thousands and a television audience of millions.

- It was a tragedy that changed the face of British football by leading to the removal of fencing round the perimeter of pitches, the abolition of massive standing areas, and the conversion of major grounds into all-seater stadia.

- It led to medical-legal history being established by a House of Lords decision that doctors could stop feeding artificially a Hillsborough victim who had been unconscious since the moment of the tragedy. On the day Tony Bland was allowed to die, three years after being crushed into a coma, Hillsborough claimed its 96th victim.

- It was also a disaster which brought the regional press of Merseyside, the Liverpool *Echo* and its sister morning paper, the *Daily Post*, into conflict with some of the national tabloids, notably the *Sun* and the *Daily Star*.

Some of the events which followed the tragedy called upon the local media to speak up on behalf of the community it served, to comfort without sacrificing objectivity. I like to think that the *Echo* did not fail the people of Liverpool when they needed support at the moment of Hillsborough, and when they needed advocacy in the continuing search for justice by the families of the bereaved.

Action stations

Let us turn back the clock in the *Echo* news room to 3 p.m. on 15 April 1989. The news editions for the day have gone. All that remains is the Football Pink. And this is going to be something special. Both the city's first division teams, as they were then, are in the semi-finals of the FA Cup. It is Liverpool against Nottingham Forest at Sheffield, and Everton versus Norwich City at Villa Park, Birmingham. There is optimism in the air that by the end of the afternoon we will all be getting ready to plan the coverage of a 'Liverton' FA Cup final at Wembley, underlining the claim that the city is the football capital of England.

Assistant news editor Bob Burns, himself an ardent Liverpool fan, hears from the sports desk that play at Hillsborough has been stopped after six minutes. The first flashes reported that supporters behind the Liverpool goal were spilling on to the pitch. About the same time television were transmitting live coverage of crowd scenes at the ground. There was no mention at that stage of anybody having been killed. It was not until 4.17 p.m. that an announcement was made by the police that the game had been abandoned because of a 'serious incident'.

Long before that, however, news had been filtering back from our own sports staff at the ground that there were casualties, some of them fatal. The alarm bells were ringing, but nobody at that time suspected the true scale of the catastrophe.

By 4.45 the *Echo* switchboard was besieged by calls from relatives of many of the fans who had travelled to Hillsborough. They were desperate for information.

Commentators on television and radio were speaking of 40 fans being killed, going up to 60 within ten minutes and reaching 74 deaths by the time the *Echo*'s football edition was ready to print.

The editor at that time, Chris Oakley, was away on a boating holiday on the Norfolk Broads and could not be contacted. It fell to those on duty, led by associate editor Vin Kelly and deputy editor Joe Holmes, to recommend that we should produce a special disaster edition for distribution on the Sunday morning. This decision was ratified by senior company management, and by 6.00 existing staff on duty had been built up to a full team, production as well as editorial.

Three or four off duty reporters had travelled to Hillsborough as Liverpool supporters or the girl friends of Liverpool supporters. Others had been at Villa Park as Everton fans, and had called in from there as news reached them that there had been a major tragedy at the other semi-final. Deputy news editor Alf Bennett and more reporters and photographers had been contacted at their homes, or, like me, had telephoned in to the office on hearing the first news flashes on radio or television.

Everybody was in position before 7.00. There was a team of 15 reporters and six photographers filing stories and pictures. They were reporting from Sheffield Wednesday's ground, the police headquarters at Sheffield, the two hospitals where casualties were being treated, the railway and coach stations in Liverpool, and from Anfield, home of Liverpool Football Club. Other reporters were based in our news room, where they were able to respond to the deluge of information coming in over the telephones from members of the public – information which brought tales of great heart-break and great heroism.

There were also expressions of anger at what many callers regarded as inadequate crowd control outside the ground, and a slow response to the developing crisis from those responsible for safety inside the Leppings Lane end.

Hillsborough was a tragedy that did not stop at the front door of the Liverpool *Echo*. It swept right into the news room. Soon we discovered, for example, that the brother of one reporter working on the story was lying in a coma among the injured; and that the cousin of another was feared – rightly – to be among the dead.

The atmosphere on the editorial floor was sombre. The adrenaline was pumping, but the bustling excitement usually associated with a big story was muted. For the first time in a long newspaper career I was seeing reporters with tears in their eyes as they helped to piece together a tragedy of epic proportions.

It was difficult to find anybody on duty over that fateful weekend who did not have a relative, friend or neighbour touched by the disaster. The victims spanned all walks of life, included brothers and sisters and ranged in age from schoolboy to grand-dad.

Probably the most difficult editorial decision we had to make that night was the choice of a picture to carry the front page of a special disaster edition we had decided to publish the next morning. It

Figure 2 Liverpool *Echo*: special Sunday edition

is one thing to print an horrific picture of an incident in another part of the world, but greater care is needed if that picture shows people from your own locality, especially if relatives and friends may not be aware of their involvement. The front page picture had to capture the enormity of the tragedy and yet not be so harrowing that it would be offensive to our readers. By some careful cropping of one picture, I think we got it right, helped by the headline 'Our Day of Tears'.

At least we escaped the barrage of criticism levelled at other papers, especially the *Daily Mirror*, the following day. They published pictures showing the plight of the trapped victims in grisly detail, and the fact that the *Mirror* was printing in colour added another dimension to the horror of their photographs.

But our decision to publish a special edition on the Sunday was not without critics. It was seen by some, including one local radio commentator, as an unseemly attempt to profit from the tragedy. Commercial considerations, in fact, could not have been further from our minds. The Sunday edition was a newsman's instinctive reaction to serve his readers as best he could at a time of great tragedy. As it turned out, the proceeds of the cover price, and an amount equal to the sum that would otherwise have been paid to staff by way of overtime, were donated to the Hillsborough Disaster Fund.

By Monday morning, Merseyside was under siege from the media. Newspapers and television companies had mobilised their big battalions. One national daily alone was said to have put a team of 20 reporters and photographers into the area. The *Echo* reports on Hillsborough were being sent round the world by fax, by telex and by telephone. Australia, New Zealand, Canada, America, Hong Kong, Scandinavia, and most other European countries were actively seeking the most up to date news. Senior members of our staff were daily giving live radio and television interviews to English speaking countries, and we were also playing host to London staff who had been moved into the area by their international agencies.

The sheer volume of media people on Merseyside at that time must have added greatly to the burden of bereaved families. It was not just the *Echo* knocking on their doors for information. It must have seemed to some as if the whole world was on their doorstep.

Newspapers are sometimes criticised at times like this for intruding unduly at the moment of deepest grief. But what critics fail to understand is that the reporter from the local paper is most often welcomed as a shoulder to cry on, a sympathetic listener, and, on occasions, as a potential ally in adversity.

The same degree of trust may not always be shown to some national newspapers. After Hillsborough we came across a handful of examples of reporters from out of town claiming to be from the *Echo*, presumably in an effort to gain the confidence of the people they were seeking to interview.

In its edition of April 21, the *Echo* printed the following statement:

> The National Union of Journalists Liverpool Branch and North Wales Area Council are looking into complaints that some national newspaper journalists masqueraded as reporters from the Liverpool *Daily Post* and *Echo*, and one as a social worker from Liverpool City Council, to obtain photographs or interviews from relatives of Hillsborough victims.
>
> We can only express our sincere regrets to bereaved relatives who have suffered the cruel consequences of any such deceit.

It is worth noting that during the week after Hillsborough, the *Echo* was refused details about victims on only half a dozen occasions. On one of those occasions the family changed their minds after seeing a photograph and details of their son's friend in the paper. They telephoned the *Echo* the next day and asked us to go back and produce a similar type of story about their own boy.

The city was still reeling from the news when allegations began to surface that drunkenness, hooliganism and the late arrival of a large body of supporters were the main ingredients of the tragedy.

The atmosphere on Merseyside was not helped when Jacques Georges, the then president of UEFA, was reported on the radio as condemning the Liverpool fans for having 'charged into the arena with the savagery of beasts'. His comments were seemingly based on a reported statement by a South Yorkshire police officer, withdrawn within minutes, that the gates at Hillsborough had been burst open by rampaging Liverpool fans. M. George's comments provoked an angry response. In a page one comment (18 April) the *Echo* called for his removal from office and described him as 'a bigot beneath contempt'.

By now it had become clear to us that there were major question marks over the way in which crowd control outside the ground had been organised and the efficiency of the stewarding inside the Leppings Lane end of the ground. There was a growing suspicion, too, that somebody was encouraging journalists to angle reports against the behaviour of the Liverpool fans.

What had been a suspicion on the Monday and Tuesday became a heart-breaking reality for the people of Liverpool the next day.

The *Echo* news room was just dumbfounded by the jumbo headlines in the *Sun* telling the country

THE TRUTH
Some fans picked pockets of victims
Some fans urinated on the brave cops
Some fans beat up PC giving kiss of life

Next came the *Daily Star* with

Dead fans robbed by drunk thugs

Our switchboard was flooded with calls from people beside themselves with anger. Many of the callers were people who had been at the heart of the rescue activities at Hillsborough. They knew from the evidence of their own eyes, they told us, that there was not a shred of truth in allegations now being presented as facts. Some of the callers were crying with anger.

The *Sun*, in particular, felt the full weight of a community outraged. Copies were publicly burned in the square of a shopping precinct at Knowsley. Shop floor workers banned the paper from factories all over Merseyside, and newsagents were asked by customers to remove it from their shelves, if they had not already done so on their own initiative.

That night (19 April) the *Echo* reflected the feelings of its readers, and of its own staff. We had probably interviewed more eye witnesses than any other paper, and nobody had seen anything remotely resembling the scenes that were now being described. Under the headline 'Speaking up for Merseyside... and for the memories of the innocents who died', the *Echo* challenged the two newspapers, and

South Yorkshire Police, to produce evidence to back up these astonishing accusations.

Figure 3 Liverpool *Echo* 19 April

Who saw what? Where were the pictures? Why had there been no arrests? These were the questions to which Merseyside was demanding answers.

The *Echo* described the allegations as a 'poisonous smoke screen' put up in a 'vile attempt to divert attention from the stark fact that inadequate crowd control led directly to the deaths of 95 innocent Liverpool supporters'.

Other newspapers had carried similar stories, some on their front pages. But none had claimed the stories to be 'the truth', and most made it clear that they were reporting non-attributable allegations, mainly from police sources.

Next day the *Sun* tried to justify itself by pointing out in its leader column that their report referred only to 'some' of the fans, while the *Star* carried a page one story headed

LIES
Cops made up tale of looting, says their angry boss

The *Echo* commented:

> the fact that in the story the Chief Constable says no such thing is apparently of small concern to a paper desperate to ingratiate itself with the people of Merseyside after yesterday's muck raking.

> The Sun and the Star – together in the gutter.

At the time of Hillsborough, the *Sun* was one of the top selling morning newspapers on Merseyside. But the decision of editor Kelvin Mackenzie to publish those wild allegations as 'the truth' cost his paper dear. In their book about the rise and fall of the *Sun* Peter Chippindale and Chris Horrie (1990) reveal the extent of that setback to a paper engaged in a fierce circulation battle on Merseyside with the *Daily Mirror*.

> The news trade being notoriously secretive about sales, completely accurate figures are always hard to come by but reliable inside estimates were soon indicating that in the area around Merseyside *Sun* sales had gone through the floor. From sales before the disaster of 524,000 copies a day, the paper had crashed to 204,000.

> News International themselves admitted to losing 40,000 readers – a drop from 140,000 to 100,000 within the central area of Merseyside.

Sales of the *Sun* have recovered to some extent since that knee-jerk protest, but it will never be forgiven by those who suffered because of

Figure 4 Liverpool *Echo* 21 April

Hillsborough. This was illustrated nearly eight years later when the paper put out a free issue as a promotion to mark the launch of the mid-week National Lottery on 5 February 1997. Radio Merseyside's phone in programme that day reported that a man walked into a newsagent's shop in Maghull, on the outskirts of Liverpool, picked up all the remaining free copies of the *Sun*, tore them into shreds and dumped them in a waste bin. Hillsborough remembered!

Mourning

The attack on the Liverpool fans occurred as preparations were being made for the first funerals of the victims of the tragedy. The weight of media coverage, and the content of some of it, had created an unusually sensitive, almost explosive atmosphere in the city.

As a result, the editors of both papers, Chris Oakley of the *Echo* and John Griffith of the *Daily Post*, decided that they would not send photographers to cover any of the funerals, even though some were being attended by public figures and all of them by players or officials of Liverpool Football Club. A joint statement by the two editors was published on the front page of the *Echo* on 20 April under the headline

THE FUNERALS
Why our cameras won't be there

The statement said

> This is a decision of our two newspapers in recognition of the scale of the tragedy and the excesses of some London papers, which have caused bitter resentment locally.

The *Echo* went on to add

> If any photographer attending a funeral of a Hillsborough victim says he or she is from the Echo or the Daily Post – do not believe them. THEY ARE LYING.

Seven years later, after the terrible shooting tragedy at Dunblane, television companies and many national newspapers withdrew cameras from the Scottish village when funerals were taking place to enable families to grieve in private. Perhaps a media lesson had been learned from Hillsborough.

Meanwhile, two of the *Echo*'s senior journalists, Gerard Henderson and Andrew Edwards, had been carrying out a detailed investigation into Hillsborough, helped by a sequence of pictures taken by a reader, Andy Jones, from a vantage point in the stand near Leppings Lane. Each picture, timed by the club clock, showed the build-up in the central pens behind the Liverpool goal at a time when there was ample space in the areas on either side. The whole package was published on the front page – and five other pages – under the headline 'Hillsborough disaster exclusive: Now the *real* truth'.

Figure 5 Liverpool *Echo* 22 April

The *Echo*'s dossier, together with prints of the pictures, was subsequently submitted to the public inquiry which had been set up under Lord Justice Taylor.

The saddest seven days in Liverpool's sporting history ended at 3.06 p.m. on Saturday 22 April, when the city observed a minute's silence, also observed by the cities of Sheffield and Nottingham, and by football crowds all over the country. 'Golden silence says it all' read the *Echo* headline on its report from Anfield, where the ground had been turned into a cathedral of mourning. The railings and terraces of the Kop were adorned with scarves and other football memorabilia, and the pitch itself was a carpet of floral tributes to those who had died. Hundreds of thousands of people visited Anfield during that week. Many of the *Echo* staff were among them, and many of us by-passed the privileged Press entrance to join the long queue that daily snaked its way along the streets surrounding the ground. It was our way of making the visit personal rather than professional.

We became part of a scene which Lord Justice Taylor described as 'poignant and moving'. His own visit to Anfield, he said, made him realise 'how deeply this community has been afflicted, and how deeply it feels its loss'.

The volume of obituary notices received by the *Echo* underlined that view. There was page after page every night, from companies, trade union branches and clubs, as well as family and friends.

The Taylor Report – and after

The public inquiry conducted by Lord Taylor exonerated the Liverpool fans from the wild accusations that had been levelled at them by the *Sun* and other papers. The *Echo* (4 August 1989), reporting on his Interim Report into Hillsborough, quoted Lord Justice Taylor as commenting

> Before this inquiry began there were stories reported in the press, and said to have emanated from police officers present at the match, of 'mass drunkenness'.

> It was said that drunken fans urinated on the police while they were pulling the dead and injured out, and others had even urinated on the bodies of the dead and stolen their belongings.

> Not a single witness was called before the inquiry to support any of those allegations, although every opportunity was afforded for any of the represented parties to have any witness called whom they wished.

As soon as the allegations I have mentioned were made in the press, Mr Peter Wright, Chief Constable of South Yorkshire, made a dignified statement dissociating himself from such grave and emotive calumnies. Those who made them, and those who disseminated them would have done better to hold their peace. (Taylor 1989)

But even this unambiguous comment did not expunge the stories from cuttings libraries supplying information to the media in many parts of the world. As a result, they come back from time to time to renew the suffering of bereaved families, survivors and of the city itself. Three years after the disaster, for example, we were sent clippings from America of a story published in the *Sacramento Bee*, a newspaper circulating in the Pasadena area of California. The paper, setting the scene for the 1994 World Cup, reproduced the original *Sun* front page over a story saying

US soccer fans are not familiar with the hooligans and drunken bums who are about to invade us.

This sort of incident, and a willingness on the part of some national media to persist in giving prominence to allegations of drunkenness and hooliganism, has left Hillsborough survivors bitter and resentful. They feel it is as if Lord Justice Taylor had never spoken. Perhaps we should remind ourselves of his words at the end of the first stage of his exhaustive public inquiry, which led the *Echo* (4 August 1989) to report that Mr. Wright had offered to resign as Chief Constable and that Superintendent David Duckenfield, in command at Hillsborough, had been suspended pending further inquiries.

Lord Justice Taylor says in his Interim Report

In all some 65 police officers gave oral evidence at the Inquiry. Sadly I must report that for the most part the quality of their evidence was in inverse proportion to their rank. There were many young Constables who as witnesses were alert, intelligent and open. On the day, they and many others strove heroically in ghastly circumstances aggravated by hostility to rescue and succour victims. They inspired confidence and hope.

By contrast, with some notable exceptions, the senior officers in command were defensive and evasive witnesses. Their feelings of grief and sorrow were obvious and genuine. No doubt these feelings were intensified by the knowledge that such a disaster had occurred under their management. But, neither their handling of problems on the day nor their account of it in evidence showed the qualities of leadership to be expected of their rank...

It is a matter of regret that at the hearing and in their submissions, the South Yorkshire Police were not prepared to concede they were in any respect at fault in what occurred. (Taylor 1989)

Lord Justice Taylor concluded that the main cause of the disaster was the failure of police control, and that in seeking to rationalise their loss of control some officers over-estimated the drunken element in the massive crowd of supporters that had been allowed to build up in the confined area of the Leppings Lane turnstiles. In answer to the question 'Was drunkenness a major factor in the crisis at the turnstiles?' he said

I am satisfied on the evidence, however, that the great majority were not drunk, nor even the worse for drink. (Taylor 1989)

You seldom see or hear these words repeated. But commentators and newspaper columnists, including Sir Bernard Ingham, have gone on blaming Liverpool's 'tanked up mob' for being the main cause of the disaster.

The comments of Ingham have a special significance. At the time of Hillsborough he was Press Secretary to Prime Minister Margaret Thatcher, and had been with her when she visited the scene and spoke to many of those involved. And here he was in the *Daily Express* five years later, writing

Ever since Lord Justice Taylor of Gosforth whitewashed the drunken slobs who caused the Hillsborough football

disaster by storming the perimeter wall I have had my beady
eye on this jurist. (Ingham 1994)

Another depressing factor has been the temptation on the part of
many of the media to link Hillsborough with the Heysel disaster four
years earlier. The hooligan element then, involving Liverpool fans, was
a significant factor in causing a wall to collapse, resulting in the deaths
of Juventus supporters.

The *Echo* (19 April, 1989) commented at the time of
Hillsborough

> After Heysel we will be judged guilty, and our innocence will
> be hard to prove. It is the English concept of justice turned
> on its head.

The judgement of Lord Justice Taylor offered hope that this
would not be the case. Expectations were raised among the bereaved
and survivors that there would be a sequel – and that justice would
not only be done but would be seen to be done. They felt let down
when the Director of Public Prosecutions ruled that a major
investigation by West Midlands Police had not produced evidence to
justify proceeding with any criminal charges. Their frustration was
compounded when the inquest jury was guided by coroner Stefan
Popper to an accidental death verdict in the case of each victim. It was
a collective verdict that the *Echo* (29 March 1991) greeted with the
comment

> families and friends of the victims are likely to believe [that]
> an inquest verdict which suggests the Hillsborough tragedy
> was just an accident only adds insult to grievous injury.

Since then there has been no significant movement on the part of
the establishment, apart from a series of out of court settlements of
compensation claims reputed to have cost South Yorkshire Police
around £40 million. One pay-out of £1.2 million has gone to fourteen
of their own officers in a Court of Appeal ruling based on 'the
admitted negligence' of South Yorkshire Police which had exposed
the officers to 'excessively horrific events as were likely to cause
psychiatric illness, even in a police officer'.

Epilogue

On 5 December 1996, a two-hour drama-documentary, *Hillsborough*, written by Liverpool playwright Jimmy McGovern, was screened on television. He spent many months researching material, talking to survivors, and studying transcripts of evidence given at the public inquiry and inquest. Richard Wells, the Chief Constable of South Yorkshire at the time the play was being researched, refused to co-operate in the making of the programme which, he felt, would serve no useful purpose.

When it was screened, McGovern and his colleagues claimed the programme had unearthed new evidence – disputed by South Yorkshire Police – that police surveillance cameras would have shown the fatal overcrowding in the central pens in time to avert the disaster. The following day the *Echo* devoted its front page to the subject under the headline

Home Secretary considers new Hillsborough probe

Three days later, when the Home Secretary was visiting Liverpool, the front page was again devoted to Hillsborough under the headline

GIVE THEM JUSTICE MR HOWARD

There was yet another twist to the Hillsborough story two months later. On 26 February 1997 Dr. Ed Walker, an anaesthetist, revealed that Philip Hammond, one of the victims he had tried to save in hospital on the day, had been alive at 3.40 p.m.

This is regarded as particularly significant as coroner Stefan Popper had refused to admit any evidence at the inquest relating to events after 3.15 p.m. He did this on the grounds that all victims had been brain dead before that time. Many of the bereaved families were angered by this ruling as it excluded evidence of how police and other emergency services responded to the disaster and treated the injured, both areas of concern and criticism.

Dr. Walker, who made a statement at the time but was not called to give evidence at the inquest, was put in touch with Mr. Hammond and the Hillsborough Support Group of families after reviewing

McGovern's play for a medical journal. The *Echo* reported his revelation under the front page banner

BREAKTHROUGH
Doctor's crucial new evidence

Dr. Walker said in an interview

> I can't believe I have been sitting on this stuff for eight years. I had no idea it was so important. (Liverpool *Echo* 1997)

At the time of the television play, Chief Constable Wells was quoted as saying that he would co-operate with a new inquiry if established, but that 'it is now time for everyone to move on'. The *Echo* took a different view in a front page comment

> Well he would, wouldn't he. The South Yorkshire Police, with its convenient early retirements and its compensation payouts, can move on. The Hillsborough families, with a burning sense of injustice, cannot.

References

Chippindale, P. and Horrie, C. (1990) *Stick it up Your Punter: the rise and fall of the Sun* London: Heinemann
Ingham, B. (1994) Comment column *Daily Express* 30 June
Liverpool *Echo* (1997) 'Doctor's crucial new evidence' 26 February
Scraton, P., Jemphrey, A. and Coleman, S. (1995) *No Last Rights: The Denial of Justice and the Promotion of Myth in the Aftermath of the Hillsborough Disaster* Liverpool: Liverpool City Council Hillsborough Project
Taylor, L.J. (1989) *The Hillsborough Stadium Disaster 15 April 1989: Interim Report Cmd 765* London: HMSO

10 A TALE OF TWO CITIES: LIVERPOOL

Paddy Marley

Let me start by saying that I am not a public relations specialist. I am not a journalist or reporter. I am not even an information specialist. I am simply a local government administrator who happened to be working in the social services department of a city which was deeply affected by a terrible tragedy.

But I had to learn how to deal with meeting the public's information needs following the Hillsborough disaster on 15 April, 1989, when 95 people lost their lives and 766 people were officially recorded as being injured. In the process I had to ensure that people's needs were met in many other respects, from covering funeral expenses to providing shoulders to cry on.

My introduction to dealing with an emergency started at 10 p.m. on that Saturday when my director telephoned me and asked me to report to headquarters on Sunday morning. Something told me I would be there for some time so I took a six-pack of milk with me, and as I did not leave the premises again until Monday evening I was proved right. Over the next three or four weeks I got four or five hours sleep per night.

Other contributors to this book concentrate on the actual scene of a disaster. However, there is another side of the disaster response which is just as important, and that relates to the ongoing information service, which requires a structured response. Here I am talking about the public's information needs, and not just the media needs. In giving you a pen picture of Liverpool Council's activities I would stress that this chapter is about responding to the disaster from Liverpool and not the actual scene at Hillsborough. Nor shall I deal with the on-site emergency situation in Sheffield.

In the context of this chapter, the public comprises three distinct sectors.

- those who read newspapers and watch television but are not directly involved in the tragedy – in other words, those with a general interest in what the media reports

146

- casualties and relatives and friends of those involved in the tragedy
- other agencies or organisations which may be drawn into the effects of the tragedy or have some association with the victims.

General media

Obviously as soon as a disaster or crisis occurs the organisation involved is bombarded by all elements of the media for information, comment and interviews. Because of the personal nature of the effects of disasters it is essential that responses to the media are organised and controlled and that 'rules of engagement' are agreed. Following Hillsborough we felt media contact was a job for one person who had to be freed from other responsibilities if the task was to be carried out effectively and efficiently.

At Hillsborough one person, the director of social services for Liverpool, was appointed as the media spokesperson for all five local authorities on Merseyside and all contact was directed through him. He was relieved of his normal departmental role which was taken on by his deputy. He was given the full-time services of a senior public relations officer who advised on presentation, content of briefings and so on. All the media were informed that there would be only one general press conference per day and all the facts and figures available would be disseminated then. This provided the basic structure for information giving and both the city council and the media could plan accordingly.

Following the daily briefings the public relations officer and the director would arrange personal interviews or visits by the media to specific sites or workplaces to demonstrate the various services being provided. In addition, the inevitable visits of VIPs formed part of his role.

Underpinning this was an operations team headed by myself – with complete authority for decision making – comprising senior officers whose function it was to monitor events, receive and collate information, and pass it to relevant agencies or workers, ensuring liaison between the nine local authorities involved: Liverpool, Sefton, Wirral, St. Helens, Knowsley, Lancashire, Cheshire, Nottingham and Sheffield. Within this unit there was also a public relations officer, who could extract the information which had a public relations or media use and ensure that this was made available to his senior colleague and the director.

It is important to note that personal details of casualties were not a matter for the local authority to handle until the police made such information publicly available. Any inquiries of this nature had to be directed to the police casualty bureaux even though we had the information being asked for. That information was only given to us so that we could plan support services, arrange for help and advice to relatives and friends, and in some cases to assist with confirmation of details.

We had two police officers allocated to us within hours of the Hillsborough disaster. Their role was to act as liaison officers with Sheffield and to provide us with information on victims, hospital admissions and discharges, which relatives had been informed of deaths and generally to assist us with any inquiries or arrangements. But the task of the police in identifying victims and notifying families, while always an unenviable one, was particularly difficult at Hillsborough and we had to be careful not to complicate their problems by any statements we made regarding casualties.

However, basic factual information received from the police and other agencies was all co-ordinated by the operations team and I would suggest that this type of unit is a pre-requisite of any planning process. The staff have the time to sift the information, verify it and ensure that it is passed on to those who need to know – be that the media spokesperson, the helpline staff, the voluntary groups or staff at drop-in centres where relatives and friends of victims congregate. The unit also provides a decision making centre which everyone is aware of, and which is available 24 hours a day.

The type of information which the media normally wanted at the daily briefings were

- number of casualties, both deaths and injured. This obviously varied from day-to-day

- what professional services were being provided by the local authorities both at the scene of the disaster and elsewhere

- what arrangements had been made for bodies both at the scene and when they were returned home

- what contacts had we established with the Football Club
- copies of any pamphlets or posters which were produced
- details of financial help available; travel arrangements to and from Sheffield; Information on the locations and opening hours of drop-in centres
- details of the trust fund
- anecdotes or details of cases of special interest which had come to light

One of the specific jobs in which the public relations staff were involved was the production of leaflets and posters which advertised the services available. This was quite a substantial task as there was a need to co-ordinate the input of specialist advisers on the content of the material and to ensure an attractive eye-catching document as the end product. However at a time of tragedy the contents of such leaflets must be examined in the light of the particular nature of the disaster, and each sentence must be scrutinised for normal phrases which could have a different meaning in particular circumstances.

A graphic example is provided in a leaflet we produced, based on one which had been published following the Bradford football stadium fire, and containing very helpful advice to those affected by disaster. Thousands of copies of the leaflet were printed and distributed through drop-in centres, libraries and other public places in Liverpool and Sheffield, to help those affected by the Hillsborough disaster to understand how they felt, so that they would be better able to acknowledge that they needed help. This is how the leaflet ends.

Don't hesitate to seek help. No problem is too big or small for us to help you deal with. **Everyone** needs help – it is nothing to be ashamed of. Anything you say will be totally confidential.

FINALLY, REMEMBER – you're the same person you were before this tragedy. There **is** a light at the end of the tunnel.

Where did most of the victims of Hillsborough die? In the tunnel on the Leppings Lane terraces.

The media are a vital part of any crisis planning process. There is an insatiable appetite for information at times of disaster and a responsible media approach can provide not only news coverage but also disseminate information on services available which we want to be made widely known as quickly as possible. This is when we use the media rather than seeing them as a hindrance to providing a service. In getting our message out they can be invaluable.

After Hillsborough we were approached not only by local and national radio, television and newspapers, but also by international agencies, including CBS and Sky, and by Italian and Dutch television, who all sent teams into the area.

There is, however, another side of the media which can be extremely destructive. That is why rules of engagement are necessary from the outset. Some media are only after the explosive headline and will pursue any avenue to obtain what they want. We had to issue completely new identity badges to 300 of our staff because some reporters were openly trying to obtain identity tags to gain access to vulnerable people and confidential information.

With the benefit of hindsight, I would say that a clear warning should be given at the outset that where underhand methods are used or victims and their families are being exploited the result will be exclusion of those members of the media from any briefings or information services. The Liverpool Branch of the National Union of Journalists sought our co-operation in sending an apology to victims' families for the activities of some of their colleagues, and gave an undertaking to take up any complaints on their behalf. I would also commend the approach of the *Daily Post* and *Echo* in Liverpool who behaved very professionally and ensured that victims were not harassed.

Where possible the media should be encouraged to be part of the response to the disaster.

It is useful to give the media controlled access to parts of the services being provided such as a helpline and drop-in centres as this helps to promote the fact that the services are available to those who need them, but this must be on a controlled basis to avoid intrusion. This approach is infinitely better than their feeling they have to resort to underhand methods to sneak into protected or vulnerable areas.

The one clear message to bear in mind with the media is that if it is happening now they are interested. If it is yesterday they lose interest. So if you want to communicate, get your message out as soon as possible.

Here is my check list for dealing with the media.

Check list

1. immediately appoint a spokesperson, who must be of director status, as the only one to deal with the media, and relieve that person of their normal duties

2. provide him/her with a senior public relations officer to give expert advice, support and guidance

3. give the media specific times and places for daily briefings when the majority of information can be disseminated

4. lay down 'rules of engagement' governing the conduct of the media and stressing that if they adopt an intrusive or exploitative approach our co-operation will be withdrawn

5. establish an operations team of senior managers to collate and present information and to research particular topics in which the media express an interest

6. personal interviews for television, radio and the press should be spread out to avoid pressure on the spokesperson.

Victims, relatives and friends

When a tragedy occurs the relatives and friends of victims initially are in a state of panic. Their first action is to contact the police casualty bureau which is normally immediately available via television and radio announcements: the numbers which are flashed across the screen during news bulletins and repeated regularly on the radio. However, until detailed information flows into that bureau the police can give little help and those affected are then left to their own devices to cope with the stress and worry. They need an additional source of information and a facility to talk to someone to share their concerns, and they need it quickly.

Hillsborough was a classic example of many disasters where there is a geographical barrier which makes relatives and friends more isolated in that they cannot easily visit the location to establish the facts. By 12.00 noon on the Sunday, the day after the disaster, we had isolated 12 telephone lines and broadcast two telephone numbers for a 24-hour helpline where people could register their worries, talk over their concerns, obtain facts about the general nature of the tragedy, and be given concrete advice on what facilities were being established to help them overcome problems. These included establishing drop-in premises where people could meet and exchange information; obtain practical help in the form of food and money; travel facilities to visit Sheffield; where necessary the arrangements for funerals; and as important as all these, the opportunity to talk for hours on end and to cry.

Drop-in centres are a particularly useful resource in that many people will not normally seek help from a social services department. Although I worked in a social services department, I am not a social worker and I certainly would not willingly invite one into my home. But if there is somewhere people can just call into without any form filling or bureaucracy they feel more able to open up. The WRVS made endless cups of tea; we provided supplies of cigarettes and tissues; counsellors moved around and sometimes introduced people who were at the scene to others whose relatives were injured. There was a very emotive atmosphere at these centres but a feeling of belonging was generated.

In practical terms there was a need for money to be available as many families were faced with funerals but they did not have any money for appropriate clothes – especially for the children. Some did not have any food in the house because the breadwinner was a victim and Social Security did not respond quickly enough in the circumstances. Some close relatives who lived far away wanted to come home and needed to have their travelling costs taken care of. We arranged for a grandmother to come back to Liverpool from Australia: she kept the family together and helped them to get over the tragedy, as well as preventing the children from having to be taken into care.

These are not normally situations which bureaucrats are faced with. In normal circumstances clearly specified procedures were laid down for authorising expenditure on specific items, but at times of tragedy organisations have to be more flexible. My operations team and I had that authority, for whatever expenditure was required to be incurred on the spot

This all happened within a day or two of the tragedy. An immediate response of this nature is an absolute necessity if more long term problems of relatives and friends feeling angry, isolated and rejected, are to be avoided.

At the same time, plans for disseminating information on a wider scale were put in hand. The leaflets and posters I referred to earlier, advising those involved of what they could expect to feel, were invaluable. In our case 50,000 of these were produced and they were distributed to the media, drop-in centres, GPs' surgeries, schools, youth clubs, football clubs and any other location where people tended to congregate. When people saw in print the advice that what they were feeling was normal it helped to counteract their ideas that they were not coping. The leaflets also helped those who were close to the victims by alerting them to irrational behaviour which would be likely to occur.

The main thrust of the information-giving exercise was to help those affected to realise that they are human and that their feelings are normal. We were already providing practical help to overcome the logistical and financial effects of the tragedy, but we wanted also to cater for the emotional effects. Information to help people understand what they can expect to feel emotionally was of untold assistance.

Some of the inquiries which arose were of a practical and emotional nature, such as the woman who rang to tell our helpline that when her husband's body was returned his clothes, and even his wedding ring, were missing.

Beyond the immediate need for information services there was a need to consider the longer term requirements, when the impact has lessened and the media have lost interest. There were still a very large number of people who were injured, were present at the scene, relatives and friends of those killed or injured who still needed a form of information service. Experience has shown that many years after a disaster the need for communication still exists.

We addressed this need after Hillsborough by producing *Interlink,* a newsletter in which people could correspond with others affected. *Interlink,* which only ceased publication in 1995, served a very useful and therapeutic purpose. It published poems, letters and recollections and had photographs and illustrations of memorials and memorabilia connected with Hillsborough. But something like that does not just appear. It requires expertise. Our public relations staff were involved in its inception but once it was established it was handed over to the victims.

Figure 6 *Interlink*

Here is my check list for dealing with victims and their relatives and friends.

Check list

1. immediately establish a telephone helpline facility staffed by experienced mature professionals who are trained to listen. There should be a minimum of 10 lines available

2. from calls received, gather information on what services and help are most in demand and organise responses accordingly. Pass all information received to the operations team.

3. the operations team must keep helpline staff fully informed of developments and information on victims and services being provided

4. as soon as possible, arrange for leaflets and posters to be printed and widely circulated, making clear to those involved what feelings and emotions they can expect to experience and what help is available: take care on wording

5. open a drop-in centre or centres, staffed by experienced professionals, where people can meet to discuss concerns, share experiences and obtain practical assistance. These should be located close to places where these people would normally congregate

6. when practical, try to organise the publication of a newsletter for those affected, where victims and casualties can express their feelings in print and also make contact with others affected. This can remove the sense of isolation where there is a geographical barrier to personal contact.

Other agencies

Each disaster is unique in its effect but a common thread is that many agencies and individuals want to be involved, offer professional expertise and financial assistance. Such offers of help poured into our helplines during the first few days and weeks, and ranged from individuals and groups offering their professional skills in counselling, social work or whatever to those who wished to offer food, clothing, holidays or some other practical help. We found that these communications had to be acknowledged, dealt with and evaluated very quickly. Offers of help and gifts tend to evaporate in a short space of time as memories fade and the initial emotion subsides.

Any practical offers which we knew from the helplines were in demand were taken up and passed on. One couple offered to give their fortnight's holiday in the Canary Islands to a victim's family; firms offered food vouchers; Marks & Spencer sent daily deliveries of sandwiches and drinks to the helpline unit and drop-in centres; printers provided material for us free of charge and out of hours.

We found that there can also be other agencies who may not even be aware that the disaster is relevant to their activities but who needed to be informed of any impact on them. For example, when disasters occur victims' immediate family members may find themselves in financial difficulties and unable to pay bills: it may be that a victim was the breadwinner. It is important therefore to notify organisations which send out bills and demands, such as council tax and housing benefit, the gas, water, electricity and telephone companies, that they should be careful not to send final demands or institute any other actions which could exacerbate the situation. This helps to protect the victims and their relatives but is also in the interests of the companies themselves, who would be pilloried as heartless and insensitive at such a time. Telephone bills, in particular, were sky high following Hillsborough.

In our case we were also faced with a large number of burials. To ensure that none of the families of victims were disadvantaged, it was agreed that the bills for all funerals would be underwritten by Liverpool Council. This offer had obvious built-in pitfalls in that some people might (and indeed did) take full advantage of the situation. Nevertheless, it was something which the leader of the council felt obliged to do.

From a communication point of view it was a considerable task. The victims, and hence the funeral directors, involved were spread throughout the country and I had no way of knowing which firm would be involved with any particular funeral. So I was faced with communicating with every funeral director. I used their national association to circulate the information and they were most co-operative, but I still spent many hours talking to individual firms regarding the arrangements for their particular funeral – many complaining that some of the bereaved were taking advantage.

To complicate matters on the information front, Liverpool Football Club had decided to have a representative at every funeral no matter where in the country the ceremony was being held. They relied on me to inform them of the name of the victim, their address, the time, date and location of each funeral and whether the cortege was leaving from the home address or some other location. As an information gathering and dissemination task this was quite a unique undertaking, but thankfully, it seemed to be successful with much credit going to the Funeral Directors' Association for ensuring that I was notified of all the details.

The final part of this section relates to the trust fund which was established immediately after the disaster. Clearly the trust fund manager was faced with an impossible task of setting up a structure capable of responding to the immediate appeals for assistance and he required support until he could establish the fund properly. Simply dealing with the money pouring in was a mammoth undertaking as over £800,000 was received by 21 April, just six days after the tragedy. Eventually it became the biggest trust fund ever, with some £12,171,488 as at 19 March 1990.

The trust fund manager initially got the local authorities to act on his behalf by agreeing to reimburse any immediate payments required by families of victims which were necessary to ensure they could manage in the short term. It would have been a mammoth task for him to communicate with every local authority, so he asked for our assistance. The operations team was working very effectively by then and so I became the liaison officer with the trust fund and was consequently seen as the information source for anything to do with that fund. Of course, most people had never been involved with such an organisation and I had to try and keep local authorities up and down the country informed of what could be done; advise various groups involved with families on how to deal with claims; try to establish facts for the trust fund manager such as accurate lists of the deceased together with details of the known injured. Eventually my information base became sufficiently accurate that the exercise became routine, and as the trust fund manager appointed his own staff, I became less involved.

Here is my check list for dealing with other agencies.

Check list

1. acknowledge, evaluate and publicise offers of help from individuals and agencies

2.   make the helpline staff aware of any offers

3.   notify gas, water, electricity, telephone and local authority agencies to check before instituting default notices

4.   if the effects involve a national network seek the co-operation of the appropriate national association in co-ordinating the response

5.   if a trust fund is established, obtain details of co-ordination.

Summary

The Hillsborough disaster occurred on 15 April 1989. Since that date the need for information of some kind or another has continued in the form of books, seminars and other events. All of the contributors to this part of the book have been asked many times to give talks, lectures and training sessions relating to their experience of the Hillsborough disaster.

The trust fund officially closed in March 1991. The co-ordinating group of local authorities wound up in May of that year and the Hillsborough telephone helpline closed down in June. Liverpool Council's Hillsborough centre ceased functioning in 1993 and, apart from the Hillsborough Family Support Group, all the other organisations or agencies involved have ceased to exist. But with each anniversary since 1989 and for some years to come, information on Hillsborough will still be sought.

I never knew anyone who was killed or injured at Hillsborough. But Hillsborough took a period of four months out of my life completely and has continued to take up time as I contribute to this book, eight years later.

I am not the same person as I was before Hillsborough and I don't think I ever will be. I shall never be rid of that tragedy.

11   A TALE OF TWO CITIES: SHEFFIELD

Shirley Harrison

At the time of the Hillsborough disaster I was the chief publicity officer at Sheffield council. This chapter aims to give the reader an idea of how we in Sheffield coped with the massive media presence in the aftermath of the Hillsborough disaster. In the process there will be a few words about the legal dimension of providing information and dealing with the media in crises and disasters. Because, from the first telephone call I took from a *News at Ten* researcher, asking me to fax them a copy of the plans of the Hillsborough football ground, until the final verdict of the coroner's court almost two years later, I had to be mindful that Sheffield council might be held to blame in some measure for what happened at Hillsborough. So in this chapter I will cover some of those legal implications from a public relations officer's point of view, as well as giving some examples of how we tried to organise ourselves and keep the media satisfied.

The disaster

I was at home that afternoon. As a life-long Sheffield Wednesday supporter I might have been at Hillsborough, but as I was not much interested in the fortunes of Liverpool or Nottingham Forest and it was a nice spring day, I was pottering about in the garden. As it happened, Philip Dent, my senior press officer and an ex-sports journalist, had just got back to his house, having taken his family out for lunch to a pub in the Derbyshire countryside.

So it was quite by chance that we were both in earshot when the first telephone calls came from the Press Association just before 4.00. I spoke to the council leader and to the chief executive and put out an official press statement via the Press Association just after 4.00. By 6.30 Phil and I had set up a base in the town hall, using my office and the adjoining one – commandeered for the purpose from the lord mayor. We had four telephones, which were in constant use until after midnight. Broadcast and press journalists calling from all over the

159

United Kingdom and abroad were in pursuit of interviews, plans of the stadium and information on ground safety. We were also acting as a clearing house for information and offers of help, and beginning to make arrangements for the launch of an appeal fund.

During the evening the I had spoken to the lord mayor, who said she wanted to set up an appeal to help those affected by the disaster, and could it be arranged as soon as possible? I had a vague recollection that funds set up in the past had had problems in distributing money because of the way in which they had been set up – how they had worded their objectives, and whether or not they had charitable status – but I was no expert on the legal niceties. The chief executive, who was a lawyer by training, gave some advice over the telephone, which I put into an appropriate form for the lord mayor's speech launching the trust the following day in Sheffield town hall.

Next morning, representatives of Sheffield, Liverpool, Nottingham and Nottinghamshire arrived at the town hall for a press conference to launch the appeal. Overnight the council's recreation department had made up wreaths and floral arrangements.

The first donation to the appeal, a beer-mug of cash collected by Nottingham Forest supporters, had already been brought into the office. The manager of the Co-operative Bank, the council's bankers, had set up an account in the name of the Hillsborough Disaster Appeal and cheques were produced by Sheffield, Liverpool, Nottingham City and Nottinghamshire County councils. Following the launch, a small civic party went to Hillsborough football ground (without the media) to deliver wreaths and then to visit the injured in the Northern General and Hallamshire hospitals. The Prime Minister also made a visit to the ground and to the hospitals during the course of the afternoon. She was accompanied by the Home Secretary, a local MP and a large contingent of the press and broadcast media.

Phil and I continued to run a limited service until late on the Sunday evening, in an effort to respond to the continuing flood of media enquiries. We also continued to act as a clearing house for all kinds of information such as offers of help in accommodating relatives, and ensuring such information was passed to the radio and television stations.

The received wisdom in crisis and disaster handling is that someone else's disaster can very quickly become your own. At

Hillsborough many different groups and organisations were rapidly affected and drawn into the tragedy. From the media and public relations point of view, these were some of them:

- Sheffield Wednesday Football Club, whose ground was chosen for the match

- Eastwood and Partners, the club's consulting engineers

- Liverpool Football Club, whose supporters were killed and injured

- the South Yorkshire police force, who were responsible for public order

- the Football Association, who were responsible for arranging the match and the ticket allocations

- Sheffield council, who had inherited the ground's safety certificate from the former South Yorkshire council

The experience of Sheffield council forms the basis for this chapter. The council's involvement on the day was slight: it had nothing formally to do with the match itself, crowd control or official representation, although both the lord mayor and the council leader happened to be at the match. But the council quickly became responsible for provision of a large mortuary; for setting up coroner's inquests; for bereavement counselling; for making arrangements to help visiting friends and relatives of those who had died or were still in hospital; for launching, organising and running an appeal fund, and making provision for a public inquiry.

Some of these were operational activities which the council was obliged to undertake. But as the area's largest employer and both the representative and the servant of the people of Sheffield, the council was both the expected provider of public information and the natural focus for media attention. The council's publicity department, as it was then called, was responsible for dealing with the media, and we took immediate responsibility for the public relations aspects of everything surrounding the disaster and its aftermath.

Some of that work was to provide information to the public, either directly or through the media. But we also undertook to satisfy the demands of the media for newsworthy material by creating and placing stories unconnected with ground safety and licensing.

The first few weeks

It was immediately plain that the council had to co-ordinate its response to the disaster and to the public information needs following on from it. Every morning before the normal day's work began, a group of council officers met briefly to clear who was responsible for saying what on a number of issues. From the news and information perspective, the purpose of these sessions was twofold: to bring everyone up to date on what had happened over the past 24 hours and to predict what was thought likely to crop up during the coming day.

On that first day, for example, we agreed that the head of the legal department would deal with safety certificates and matters concerning the licensing of the ground; the director of environmental health would field questions about post mortems and inquests; the principal safety officer would talk to the Health and Safety Executive and deal with anything on the physical attributes of the football ground; the director of social services would deal with questions about practical assistance to relatives and bereavement counselling and my staff would deal with everything else – and with co-ordination. The meetings were usually over within less than half an hour, when everyone could go about their business confident that they were clear about who was the authoritative source on each issue. The system also made clear organisationally that certain named individuals had the responsibility of talking to the press, so that everyone who did not could get on with their jobs.

It took some of the pressure off many officers who were at breaking point, without having to cope with reporters camping on their doorstep. Because it is at those moments of severe pressure that people are liable to say something which everyone might later regret. By fielding spokespeople who could cope confidently with being interviewed, we managed to avoid that danger. As far as I can remember, we never got into a muddle about this, so I can safely recommend it as a way of keeping lines uncrossed.

There was clearly going to be a hiatus of some weeks before the opening of any formal inquiry and we knew that the news media would not quietly go away and wait for proceedings to start. So we established a regular flow of information to reporters, trying to ensure that they never went away empty-handed, even if there were some topics on which we could not provide the answers the journalists were looking for. As it happened, the progress of the appeal fund provided a mass of newsworthy material which continued to be used until after the investigations closed.

Later that Monday morning, 17 April, the city treasurer and I went to Liverpool to sort out the organisation of the appeal fund. While the civic leaders had launched the Hillsborough Disaster Appeal, Liverpool Football Club had launched the Liverpool FC Relief Fund and a further fund had been launched by the Nottingham Building Society at its home base. We agreed to merge these into the Hillsborough Disaster Appeal, with a common logo, while retaining the separate bank and building society accounts. In due course, the accounts were merged. The objective of this meeting was to get the trust arrangements clarified and operational so that beneficiaries could be helped as soon as possible. As Paddy Marley says in Chapter 10, if the breadwinner had gone to the match with his wage packet in his pocket and not returned, there would be a hungry as well as a grieving family.

Figure 7 Hillsborough Disaster Appeal logo

We subsequently dealt with all aspects of the appeal from the Sheffield end, including a city-wide collection, co-ordination of events, distribution and collection of collecting receptacles (buckets and election boxes were pressed into service as well as over 1000 tins), and publicising the appeal though posters, stickers and the media. About 15 members of staff were involved at one time or another, together with a number of volunteer helpers who presented themselves at the reception desk and offered to do anything necessary.

I instituted a daily lunch time meeting with three of the team so that we could keep track of what was happening. We were fully committed on post-Hillsborough work for the first two weeks. The press team continued to answer queries from the media and also began to put out statements and releases.

In the first two weeks we dealt with a tremendous volume of enquiries from newspapers, radio and television not only in this country but also from Europe, the United States, Australia and New Zealand, dealing with all aspects of the council's involvement. We also carried out a large number of interviews ourselves, both live and recorded, on the setting up and running of the appeal fund.

Many of the donations to the appeal came by post addressed simply to the Lord Mayor, Sheffield, and most of these came with a letter or a note of some kind, which all had to be carefully read. Some told stories of the sender's own misfortunes, some wanted messages passed to bereaved relatives, but some contained information of interest to the public inquiry such as letters from people who had been at the ground on the day. These were passed to West Midlands Police, who were conducting investigations.

A Book of Remembrance, a massive leather-bound volume, was set up in the foyer of the town hall and people were invited to record messages of sympathy. Over 20,000 local people queued up to sign it. But it also had some more unexpected signatories, ranging from royalty to footballers, from civic dignitaries to snooker stars (the World Snooker was on at the Crucible across the street from the town hall and most of the players signed the book) and representatives of our own and foreign governments. Each provided an opportunity for positive media coverage, and the press team always tried to ensure that photo opportunities were created, for example, by asking football teams to come and sign dressed in their strip. These activities, while not set up with the sole purpose of getting media coverage, did help journalists to fill some of their time and space with non-damaging, non-speculative reporting.

There were other events – again, not set up for media coverage, but which could provide material for the media. These included a memorial service held at Sheffield Cathedral on 23 April and the one-minute silence, reported in Figure 8. At six minutes past three on Saturday 22 April, exactly one week later, all the traffic stopped in the centres of Liverpool, Sheffield and Nottingham, and each stayed silent for a minute.

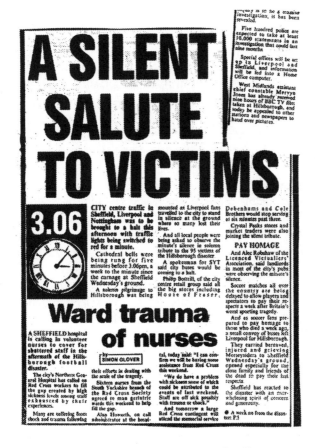

Figure 8 Sheffield *Star* 22 April

During this period the city was hosting a high level civic delegation from its twin town of Anshan in China, including Anshan's new mayor. Although their programme had to be altered because of the disaster, it was not curtailed. The visitors from Anshan signed the Book of Remembrance and attended the service held in Sheffield

Cathedral on 23rd April. In addition to arranging for a civic party to attend the service, arrangements were also made to accommodate the deputy mayor of Bochum, Sheffield's twin town in Germany. Sheffield's lord mayor had been planning a civic visit to Bochum the following week, but had of course cancelled the arrangements. Bochum's deputy mayor flew in with a substantial donation to the appeal and attended the service in Liverpool cathedral.

A Hillsborough helpline was also set up, based at Hillsborough library. It was run by an information officer who was normally responsible for the Winter Hotline, an advice service to help the elderly. The helpline was very busy during its first few days of operation dealing with people wanting to find out if relatives or friends had been involved in the tragedy, survivors who wanted to contact local people who helped them in the immediate aftermath, requests for counselling from people who had suffered trauma from the event, enquiries about the appeal fund, and many offers of assistance including transport between Sheffield and Liverpool for survivors and bereaved families, and accommodation in Sheffield. The helpline was staffed by the same volunteer helpers who usually staffed the council's Winter Hotline, and by staff at the library.

The normal working of the publicity department continued as far as possible, with all staff playing their part, notwithstanding a constant stream of camera crews, volunteers, donors, telephone and personal enquiries on a daily basis, together with visits from VIPs who appeared without warning to see how the appeal was progressing. In the main staff were glad to give their time voluntarily, putting in many extra hours at evenings and weekends.

Within a few weeks of the disaster it was clear that the department had somehow to get back to normal working. Staff were tired, stressed and emotionally affected by the work they had been doing. On 24 May we took on Roy Dixon, a former bank official, as a temporary co-ordinator for a period of three months. His main job was to deal with all the work surrounding the appeal, which then stood at £4 million, but he also kept tabs on everything else to do with the aftermath of the disaster. His appointment took the pressure off the staff in the department who had been striving to cope with the avalanche of paperwork in the wake of the disaster appeal's launch, as well as dealing with all the media calls and their normal volume of work.

The co-ordinator dealt with all the correspondence; made appropriate acknowledgements; provided details to the council leader on other local authorities who had contributed to the appeal fund (there were many); kept in touch with the trust fund manager and drew his attention to donations of over £1000 which the Inland Revenue needed to know about; and liaised with West Midlands Police about correspondence from those who said they were at Hillsborough at the time of the disaster and therefore may have been witnesses.

He also took on the task of co-ordinating all current and future activities in relation to the appeal and receiving presentations of donations in various parts of the country. He kept in constant touch with the media and ensured that all official presentations received press coverage. He also dealt with countless enquiries about the appeal and the public inquiry and gave help to others with their fund-raising activities. A massive fund-raising operation was underway on Merseyside at the same time, and he was in regular contact with his opposite numbers there. He took over the arrangement made by the press team that at 10.00 each morning they would ring round the banks and building societies which were dealing with donations and then agree with the Liverpool press office on the total figure to be released to the media that morning, in time for the first editions of our local evening press. Later in the day he would provide human interest stories for both local and national news consumption.

His final job was to arrange for Sheffield's lord mayor to present the city's Book of Remembrance to Liverpool Football Club. The presentation took place at Liverpool's first match of the new football season at Anfield on 19 August.

We continued to advise the trustees of the appeal fund on advertising and media relations, accompanying them to Hillsborough football ground and later to a 'thank you' tea with the lord mayor for those who had helped with the appeal. Although the media were not normally allowed into the lord mayor's parlour, it proved valuable to break with tradition on this occasion, acting as both a morale booster for staff, and an opportunity for the trustees to say on television what they were doing with the money raised.

At the end of August the various separate bank accounts were wound up and consolidated into the main fund account and final contacts were made with the trust fund manager and Liverpool council's appeals office and shop. When it closed the appeal fund stood at over £12 million.

Investigations and inquiries

One of the tasks of my team was to monitor the media. On 17 April we heard the then Home Secretary Douglas Hurd announce to parliament that an inquiry was to be held with the following terms of reference

> to inquire into the events at Sheffield Wednesday football ground on 15 April 1989 and to make recommendations about the needs of crowd control and safety at sports grounds.

Following consideration of a number of venues with Home Office officials, it was agreed that the public inquiry would take place in Sheffield's town hall. The council chamber and a number of committee rooms were made available to Lord Justice Taylor, who was appointed to lead the inquiry. These rooms were normally in constant use by members and officers of the council so council business had to be re-arranged.

The public inquiry began on 15 May. Oral hearings concluded on 29 June and the inquiry closed on 14 July. Lord Justice Taylor gave an interim report in time for the opening of the new football season. The press team made all the arrangements with the media and the Central Office of Information for press facilities during the inquiry. During the course of the inquiry the press office provided an ongoing facility to the media and continued to co-ordinate the council's response. We issued press releases at the close of the inquiry, on publication of the interim report at the beginning of August, and when the final report was published.

Following the inquiry the Director of Public Prosecutions decided that there would be no criminal proceedings. The inquest, which had been opened to allow release of the deceased for burial and then adjourned until the inquiry was complete, was resumed and the final verdict of accidental death was returned on the victims on 28 March 1991 – at six minutes past three.

The police inquiry internal to South Yorkshire Police continued for some time after that, held up by the illness and then retirement of officers concerned. The police force's insurers paid out compensation to the bereaved and injured. Sheffield Wednesday Football Club and Eastwood and Partners, their consulting engineers, made a contribution to that compensation. The settlements were made out of court.

The behaviour of the media

The Hillsborough disaster generated massive media coverage for many weeks after the event. There was considerable debate from the start about the way in which events were reported and sectors of the media took opposing views on what stance to take.

Ian Clarke, a survivor of Hillsborough, claimed when giving evidence to the public inquiry that a journalist posing as a hospital chaplain had to be ejected by hospital authorities, that two BBC journalists posed as his aunt and uncle to get access to the ward and that photographers tried to take pictures of the injured from a helicopter hovering outside the ward window. Paddy Marley in Liverpool social services department had to issue new identification to all his staff because reporters were trying to obtain the badges so that they could pose as social workers and gain access to bereaved relatives and to confidential information.

The local newspapers in Liverpool and Sheffield, neither of which normally published on Sundays, produced special editions on Sunday 16 April. The Liverpool *Echo* was criticised by the local radio station for doing so, on the grounds that the *Echo* was seeking to make money out of publishing a special edition. In fact, the proceeds of the cover price were donated to the appeal, and the paper carried no paid-for advertising. The Sheffield *Star*, along with a number of other newspapers, was criticised on grounds of taste and sensitivity for printing close up pictures of identifiable dying or dead victims.

Many of these criticisms found their way to the regulatory body at that time, the Press Council. In all, the Press Council examined 349 written complaints naming 35 national and provincial newspapers. One of these was in the form of a 7000 name petition from

Merseysiders, complaining about an 'unbalanced and misleading' article on the front page of the *Sun,* headlined 'The Truth', which alleged that drunken Liverpool fans had robbed victims and abused the police. As Alf Green has described in Chapter 9, the reaction in Liverpool was intense: copies of the paper were publicly burned and many newsagents refused to continue to stock it. The paper's then editor, Kelvin Mackenzie, subsequently acknowledged that he had made a serious error, but the *Sun*'s circulation on Merseyside never fully recovered.

On the other hand, both Sheffield's radio stations, BBC Radio Sheffield and Radio Hallam, were singled out for praise in a debate in the House of Commons on 17 April with MP Richard Caborn making specific references to the part they played in helping to co-ordinate the efforts made by Sheffield people in, for example, blood donation and other services, and the arrangements between the Liverpool and Sheffield families. Local radio showed what 'magnificent assistance' it can give in a tragedy.

The local media have to live with their communities, and are usually more sensitive than the national or foreign press and broadcasters, who cover the story and move on. This was well illustrated by the example of the Liverpool *Echo*, which took an editorial policy decision not to send photographers to the funerals of the victims. They risked upsetting bereaved families who may have felt snubbed because they did not see pictures of their corteges in the local paper. Their reasoning was based on two factors: they did not want to be seen to intrude on family grief with cameras; and they were able to reassure their readers that any reporter with a camera attending a funeral and claiming to be from the *Echo* would be lying.

Legal implications

There is clearly a legal dimension to public information in crises and disasters. Because the United Kingdom does not have a state no-fault compensation scheme, there is a need for someone to be sued, or found guilty of an offence, or proved negligent, before compensation can be paid to the victims. Hence the 'say nothing' instruction from insurers, handed out as advice to motorists with their policies.

There is always bound to be a tension between an organisation's public relations staff and its legal advisers as to what may be said and when. The public relations approach is generally to give as much information as possible, or at least, as is politic, as soon as that information is available. One problem is that the facts as they are known at one point in time may not bear much resemblance to the truth as it finally emerges: by then the damage may be done and beyond repair.

The legal process of public inquiry, criminal inquiry, coroner's inquest, civil cases and appeals, and internal inquiries within organisations such as the South Yorkshire Police went on for years after the event and, at the time of writing have not been concluded yet. From the point of view of the victims' relatives and those who sympathise with them, the legal process has been unsatisfactory in providing information on what really happened and why the victims died. Those most closely involved have been compelled to re-live Hillsborough several times over as they gave or listened to evidence at the public inquiry and coroner's inquest. This double trauma has at last been recognised, with the announcement that the Home Office plans to put a stop to the overlap in the system (*Civil Protection* 1997a).

The lengthy legal processes following Hillsborough established the names of the people who died and the medical cause of death in each case; the time, place and circumstances in which the injury occurred, that is as a result of a crush injury at Hillsborough football ground; and that they died accidentally. Small wonder that, with so many questions unanswered, the Hillsborough disaster continues to be the subject of controversy. As Alf Green's *Epilogue* explains, journalists – from the *Echo* and other papers – will continue to ask questions and report stories about Hillsborough, for the foreseeable future.

Turning to the Hillsborough disaster appeal, there was an element of luck involved in getting the wording right when announcing an appeal so soon after the tragedy. In the end, two trusts were set up: a discretionary trust and a charitable trust. The discretionary trust could pay out money as it chose and would not be constrained by legal definitions of poverty or need, but it would be liable to tax. The charitable trust would have tax relief and would be able to take donations from bodies who would not otherwise be able to give.

Another issue arises as to the suitability of an organisation which may ultimately be found blameworthy becoming involved in raising money for the victims of the disaster. Although Sheffield council did not find itself in this position, we judged at the start that it was particularly important that the lord mayor, a 'neutral' civic dignitary, mount the appeal. But a decision not to respond immediately would in any case have raised questions.

We climbed a very steep learning curve in the days and weeks following the Hillsborough disaster. We had formerly relied on the framework of the council's plan for peacetime emergencies and the ability of staff to cope with whatever cropped up. After Hillsborough we took a long look at our procedures and made some immediate changes. These included media training for non-public relations staff, better communications hardware and a duty system. In the longer term I re-thought the council's public relations strategy and completed the change from a 'publicity' department to a corporate in-house public relations consultancy.

I had been helped and supported by the many offers of practical advice and assistance given within days by other local authorities. Letters, phone calls and faxes from Bradford, Dover and Newbury councils gave advice, following the experiences of those districts in responding to the Valley Parade football ground fire, the sinking of the *Herald of Free Enterprise* and the Hungerford massacre.

With the support of a new chief executive, I also undertook to pass on the lessons learned by my authority to other organisations which might some day find themselves in a similar situation. As others have found, there are problems in talking openly about what one did or did not do, should or should not have done, but the council felt that the principle of disseminating best practice, or, to put it another way, learning from another's mistakes, is of over-riding importance.

References

Civil Protection (1997a) 'Plans to ease double trauma' Number 43, London: Home Office

Sheffield *Star* (1989) Page one lead, 22 April

12 THE MANAGEMENT OF AN ORGANISATION IN CRISIS

Peter Hayes

My purpose is to tell you about my involvement with the Hillsborough football tragedy which in turn resulted in considerable crisis within the South Yorkshire Police. Rather than dwelling on the disaster in detail, I will be covering the organisational problems which developed and how these were managed.

The South Yorkshire force is, and was at the time of the disaster, one of 43 in England and Wales, one of six metropolitan forces and the ninth largest police force in England and Wales. The establishment including civilian staff was a little over 4000 and the population served about 1.3 million. Local industry had been for many years concerned with heavy engineering and the production of coal and steel. Job losses in recent years from coal and steel amount to about 80,000. At the time of Hillsborough the force was described by other chief constables as 'hardy'. It was well used to dealing with major events and unpredictable situations.

There are five league football grounds in South Yorkshire, including Hillsborough which is located in Sheffield. During the past 15 years, eight Football Association semi-final cup matches have been played at this ground. At the time of the disaster the force was superbly led by the then Chief Constable, Peter Wright. Its media and public relations facilities were first class and in use every day. But despite all these strengths, in a Hillsborough situation, staff across the force – police and civilian – felt confused, hurt and vulnerable.

The tragedy

The FA cup semi-final between Liverpool and Nottingham Forest was held at the Hillsborough football ground on 15 April 1989. The kick-off was arranged for 3 p.m. and took place at that time. It was an all-ticket match – a sell-out – and 54,000 tickets had been sold. The corresponding semi-final between these same two teams had been played at Hillsborough in 1988 when the arrangements, largely identical to those in 1989, had been successful.

Before the match started there was a serious crowd build-up outside the Leppings Lane turnstiles, mainly involving Liverpool fans. This caused severe crushing and great distress to spectators including children at the front of the crowd, many of whom were in obvious danger of serious injury or worse.

Senior police officers at the turnstiles requested the ground commander to authorise the opening of an emergency gate adjacent to the turnstiles, in order to save lives. He gave that order, thus allowing fans onto a concourse area between the turnstiles and the back of the terraces and the West Stand. Many of the spectators went down a central tunnel under the stand leading to the spectator terrace area, immediately behind the goal, which was already full. A safety barrier collapsed resulting in the deaths of 95 spectators and many hundreds were injured.

A massive rescue attempt followed involving all the emergency services, the local authority and others.

On that fateful afternoon I was off duty at home, working in my garden, aware that the match was taking place and that over 1000 officers were on duty in connection with the event – 800 in and around the ground. I was called in from the garden just after 3.00 to watch television coverage of the match, when I saw fans climbing out of the Leppings Lane terrace onto the pitch, a number of apparently unconscious fans on the pitch, and police officers and others attempting resuscitation.

I telephoned the police headquarters operations room, to be told it was known that some fans had died but that the numbers and cause were at that time unknown. I immediately changed and drove to police headquarters, arriving at 3.45, the first chief officer there. The Chief Constable arrived at about 4.00, by which time it was known that more than 60 spectators had died and many were injured.

The Chief Constable and I brain-stormed through the actions which needed to be taken at the ground and at police headquarters. I checked that the major incident plan had been successfully activated and spent the next 30 minutes talking with senior operational, communications, administrative and personnel staff, all of whom needed decisions on a large number of matters.

In the next few hours the Chief Constable visited the ground, the temporary mortuary, local hospitals and the casualty bureau. He spoke personally with many national and local civic dignitaries and others, including other chief constables, offering help and asking for direction.

At about 5.00 a number of senior officers who had been on duty at the ground came to police headquarters. They were all severely shocked. I started working with them to determine more clearly what had occurred. I was aware that at this time it had been confirmed that 95 people had died; and that most of the bodies were at the temporary mortuary, set up in the gymnasium at the ground. Medical staff (many of whom were volunteers) were on hand and had rendered first-aid on a massive scale. Several hundred spectators had been injured, many seriously, and a number were in intensive care. The match had been abandoned and most of the fans had left the ground. Some officers involved were already traumatised.

Having spent time in the force operations room and seen the problems there caused by the unprecedented level of activity and demands, and spoken to senior officers and others in various parts of the force area who were involved with the incident in different ways, I soon became aware that a degree of organisational instability was occurring and seemed to be increasing. I sensed this through the clear difficulties some people were having with confidence, certainty and morale. There was clearly a need within the organisation for some kind of focal point to which people could relate generally, where they could pass on important information, share problems, get decisions – and these decisions needed to be consistent across a wide span of contemporaneous activity. In short, I became aware of a clear and urgent need for a central point of contact around which the massive interrelated organisational activity concerned with the football disaster rescue operation could be organised. This 'single focal point' would, I thought, act as a kind of psychological anchor and provide a first step towards the restoration of an improved degree of direction, balance and stability.

I decided to try and act as that single focal point and made the decision to remain at police headquarters, where I was readily accessible to everyone, to receive information, make decisions, authorise expenditure, deal with the mounting queries from both within and outside the force and as part of all of this to try and create an improved degree of stability and to support and encourage people generally. Furthermore, even from this early point, I would be able to consider the longer term implications, not least recovery to normality, investigation as to the cause of the disaster, information capture, welfare needs, legal liability and media queries.

The effects on people and the welfare response

The impact of Hillsborough in terms of emotional distress was for many, including police officers, very severe.

At the start of the tragedy a small number of officers were inches away from fans who were clearly suffering very great distress and, despite strenuous efforts, the officers were, in the short term, completely unable to help because of the pencil thin wire fence which separated them from the fans. Some afterwards experienced overwhelming feelings of helplessness, anger and guilt which haunt many of them to this day.

Shortly afterwards these same officers were helping or carrying fans on to the pitch, giving immediate first aid, and in some cases attempting resuscitation, often to no avail. Some then accompanied bodies to the temporary mortuary where they worked until the early hours of the following day, on occasions meeting with friends and relatives of the deceased who, understandably, were themselves shocked, angry and resentful. Their task in total was truly awful.

On the day of the tragedy, as senior officers involved returned to headquarters, I was generally their first point of contact. For many weeks I continued to work with officers who had been involved. I saw clear signs of great distress including withdrawal, depression, insomnia and obvious difficulty in concentrating or working effectively. In some cases these symptoms were very severe. They affected people at all levels in the organisation, including civilian as well as police staff.

From the day of the disaster the force fully utilised its internal and external welfare support and counselling services. Welfare staff were in the ground during the rescue operation and psychological de-briefing was occurring at and around the ground within a few hours of the tragedy happening. The force welfare officer, Penny Grimshaw, led this response. She worked unceasingly for many days, did not go home for a week and continued to the point of complete exhaustion, such was the level of demand for these services. Shortly afterwards, additional welfare assistance was provided from a neighbouring force, West Yorkshire, whose assistance proved invaluable.

As part of the welfare response, within hours of the tragedy everyone in the force, whether involved or not, was served with a formal notice telling them of unusual feelings and symptoms they might experience because of what had occurred. This explained that, in these circumstances, such symptoms were quite normal, and advised what they could do if the symptoms persisted or they felt they needed assistance. For many days after this officers queued outside the welfare office in police headquarters seeking help.

In the following days, the Chief Constable visited all the main police stations at shift changeover times and spoke to officers to reassure and comfort them and tell them of his understanding and support. Additionally, together with other chief officers and the welfare officer, he attended welfare seminars around the force where they met with relatives and friends of serving officers to listen to their problems and give help and advice. These were all well attended. A number of relatives and friends attended the same talks at different venues which indicated the level of anxiety they were experiencing. Almost 300 officers, as well as partners, received help from the welfare department as did some relatives of deceased and injured spectators. The effects continued to be felt: in April 1994, Richard Wells, the new Chief Constable, wrote in the local press that on average three police officers a week were leaving the force because they were haunted by the Hillsborough disaster (Sheffield *Star* 1994).

The long term implications

For most people, recollections of the Hillsborough tragedy focus upon the events of the day, Saturday 15 April 1989. From a senior management point of view, there is a greater need to consider carefully the longer term implications, which need to be both understood and managed well. Those in which I was deeply involved from the day of the disaster were the public inquiry, civil liability and criminal investigations, and the inquest proceedings.

As the South Yorkshire Police had been responsible for policing the event and were subject to criticism from day one the Chief Constable did not consider it appropriate that his force should conduct the longer term inquiry into the causes; they of course commenced an investigation on the day. On the day following, 16 April 1989, he asked the Chief Constable of the West Midlands Police to undertake this investigation, and he agreed.

The Public Inquiry

On 17 April the Home Secretary appointed Lord Justice Taylor to conduct a public inquiry into the disaster. It was decided the West Midlands Police would report directly to Lord Justice Taylor.

Very simply, the public inquiry was a shock. The South Yorkshire Police had no previous experience whatsoever to draw on. Having sought legal advice, their understanding was that the purpose of the inquiry was to discover three things: first, what happened, second, the causes, and third, to make recommendations in an effort to prevent such a tragedy occurring again, but that it was not concerned with the allocation of blame. In the light of this the officers who were to be called to give evidence were advised to be as helpful as possible.

To assume that blame is not an issue for the public inquiry is an over-simplification. From the beginning it was clear that the primary intention of the many counsel involved was to protect the interests of their clients, and they did this by attempting to cast blame elsewhere. The inquiry process can be very rigorous and on occasions severely distressing to those involved. Anyone appearing before such an inquiry needs to be prepared for this.

The fact that police officers were familiar with court proceedings and the rules of evidence was in some ways a disadvantage, as they tended from habit to operate within these limitations. Others did not. At a public inquiry the rules about statements are different. Hearsay and speculation are routine, and at times encouraged. A further problem is that afterwards others, including the courts, tend to take the inquiry report and its findings as evidence, starting their examination from that position. If, as a party to such proceedings, you disagree with that assumption, then you have to plead that point and this can be difficult.

The Taylor inquiry concluded that

> The immediate cause of the gross overcrowding and hence the disaster was the failure, when gate C was opened, to cut off access to the central pens which were already over-full.

The main cause of the disaster was the failure of police control. (Taylor 1989)

Criminal Liability

Lord Justice Taylor published his interim report on 4 August 1989, which included the observations on causation quoted above. On that same day the Chief Constable sent a copy to the Director of Public Prosecutions and asked him to consider the question of criminal liability. The Director in turn asked the West Midlands Police to conduct a criminal inquiry on his behalf. The inquiry, which considered the question of criminal culpability against anyone, not only police officers, was very thorough. It involved obtaining, collating and considering 9560 questionnaires, 5341 statements, 2392 sets of documents, 71 hours of video recordings and the transcripts of 174 persons who gave evidence to the Taylor inquiry.

A year later, on 30 August 1990, the Director of Public Prosecutions announced his decision that there was insufficient evidence to justify criminal proceedings against any officer of the South Yorkshire Police or any other person for any offence. Some of the police officers who had been waiting for this decision found the uncertainty traumatic in the extreme. One had been suspended from duty since 4 August 1989.

I notionally added the words 'at this time' to the director's decision. This was because I knew that court and other proceedings would follow, all of which would be attended by lawyers representing other parties. New evidence would be given and thus the situation with regard to criminal liability could change. In fact it did not.

Civil Liability

After the publication of the public inquiry report the South Yorkshire Police were advised by their lawyers that they would have to accept a degree of civil liability for what had occurred. The Chief Constable and the police authority decided on an out of court settlement. This was done in part to try and ensure that those whose claims were accepted would receive compensation without undue delay. This decision did not include all claimants and a number of court cases followed, three of which ended in appeals to the House of Lords. This process went on for years after the event.

Such litigation is expensive, complex and for those concerned at times intensely stressful. Psychologists advised that reliving the event, as many do when involved in protracted court hearings at these times, can – in terms of emotional pain – be as severe as was the original experience.

Inquest proceedings

An inquest hearing was held shortly after the tragedy to allow for funeral and related arrangements as necessary. A second hearing took evidence as to the cause of death and position of the bodies. The coroner made it clear that he would not finalise the inquest proceedings, which were effectively a second inquiry into the cause of the 95 deaths, until the Director of Public Prosecutions had made his decision and any criminal trials – there were none – had been finalised.

The full inquest hearing was convened in Sheffield on 19 November 1990 before Mr. Stefan Popper, HM Coroner. It was finalised on Thursday 28 March 1991. This was possibly the longest running inquest in English history. The court sat for 93 days over a total of 19 weeks. 520 witnesses were examined and 540 exhibits referred to. The final transcripts amounted to 3.6 million words.

The jury concluded with a verdict of accidental death in respect of all 95 who had died. Whilst this brought considerable relief to some of the South Yorkshire police officers who had been involved, it caused anger and resentment amongst many representing the deceased who considered an unlawful killing verdict would have been appropriate. This is understandable. Giving evidence at the inquest caused many people – including police officers – considerable anguish as they remembered painful experiences.

Conclusions and Recommendations

Planning

Senior managers and others in organisations with specific responsibilities for safety have a clear moral and legal obligation to identify predictable hazards and to plan to avoid these or minimise their impact should they happen. This point was well made in the Taylor Report which states.

The Operational Order and police tactics on the day failed to provide for controlling a concentrated arrival of large numbers should that occur in a short period. That it might so occur was foreseeable and it did. (Taylor 1989)

Failure to anticipate and adequately plan for predictable risks may well render those in authority liable for a breach of a legal duty of care. If the degree of negligence is sufficiently high then a conviction for corporate manslaughter can follow. This means that even if a person was not at the scene when the event occurred, if their responsibility to plan for this is clear, the breach of that equally so and the degree of negligence sufficiently high, conviction may follow.

The part I played at Hillsborough has been described as the 'Anchor Man role' by an academic who made a study of Hillsborough and similar events. This function can always be considered as part of the planning process.

The role was interesting. It was possibly because of my knowledge of and interest in organisational behaviour that I sensed early the problem of instability I have described. I concluded there was an immediate need for someone to adopt and maintain a central pivotal role, to act as a kind of anchor to which others could relate and in a sense tie on to as a first step towards gaining an improved sense of self-control and direction. I deliberately adopted that role, and now consider this essential whenever problems of this magnitude occur. I believe it needs to be pre-planned and the individual(s) concerned carefully chosen.

An essential need for whoever undertakes this role is to consider from the outset what the longer term implications might be and to prepare for these. For example, the possible damage to the image of the organisation, the emotional overload problems on staff, media demands, the possibility of a public inquiry, criminal inquiry, civil proceedings, inquest and in the case of the police, or similar bodies, formal discipline proceedings. Senior managers must be persuaded not to over-react notwithstanding the pressures on them and instead behave in a way which is sensible, balanced, reasonable, empathetic and professional. They must never try to avoid in any way the responsibilities both they and the organisation have.

In my experience, this responsibility can last for months and possibly years. Essentially it is to carefully and deliberately manage the organisation's response to the crisis in the longer term, anticipate as soon as possible matters which will have to be pursued over time, and start to deal with these early; to collate all these issues and keep the momentum of this longer phase flowing; and to advise colleagues, many of whom will be under considerable strain, of the further demands which may be made on them so they can be prepared, not least mentally. Such a role is absolutely necessary, not only for the reasons mentioned, but also to ensure that someone specific has responsibility for dealing with and concluding these often residual matters – which will sometimes continue over years – and which with the passage of time may become neglected.

An anchor man needs to be someone of sufficient seniority to represent the organisation, usually without reference elsewhere, and with the personality to make things happen, sometimes in a very short time scale. This is ideally a strong and self sufficient individual but one who is sensitive and empathetic at the same time. At times of severe organisational crisis, this role is, in my opinion, vital.

Objectivity

At the beginning, when confusion and uncertainty are especially high, those with a managerial role must avoid becoming entangled in the detail or over-concentrating on any one aspect of the incident. Instead, the initial need is to work hard at recognising and properly understanding the problems arising: to get a proper grasp of the overall picture in terms of the size, extent, severity, likely duration and possible impact of the incident on the organisation and the staff who will become involved.

Those same managers and supervisors need, as far as they can, to act calmly, and to be at all times decisive and positive. At the beginning they must avoid any hint of scapegoating. This is bound to occur soon afterwards, but is unhelpful in the short term. With the benefit of hindsight – which of course they do not have – it will often be said they could have acted differently or in some way better, but provided their actions were considered, well motivated and sincere, even if the criticism is valid, they will have done their best and be satisfied with that. This is important, as retrospective self-analysis can ruin people.

Welfare

Following Hillsborough some police officers had suicidal thoughts. Unusual behaviour such as the burning of uniforms, the repetitive cleaning of clothes, showering and changing many times daily were common. Dreaming of one's own death, of attending one's own funeral; of one's family dying, and similar nightmares were experienced. A few officers became mentally ill. Many will never be the same persons they were before the disaster occurred and I am probably one of these. Officers experienced a serious degree of stress, resulting in dysfunctional work performance, which was for a time a serious and widespread problem.

Welfare support needs to be available from the beginning and is of immense importance. This needs to be pre-planned and comprehensive. Many organisations have their own welfare services dealing with marital problems or work-related difficulties but usually the staff involved are neither experienced nor trained in crisis counselling. Consideration should be given to providing relevant training. In the short term assistance can very probably be provided by the local authority. This was certainly the case at Hillsborough, and the help and professionalism of all those involved was in every way impressive.

At these times managers must 'think welfare', including what might be needed for those not directly involved, especially families. They need to be generous with their help, encouragement advice and support. Problems will continue into the long term and the planning must reflect this. Professional help can be obtained in a number of ways, including on a standby basis by way of contract. It is sometimes of value to arrange mutual aid schemes with other organisations and this too should be considered.

Leadership

At times such as these recovery to normality is much influenced by the leadership forthcoming from within. In this regard the South Yorkshire Police was singularly fortunate. Peter Wright was, in my opinion, not only an outstanding leader but also possibly the most able and professional chief constable then serving. One indication of this was that during that year, 1989, he had been asked by his chief officer colleagues nationally to represent them as the president of their professional body the Association of Chief Police Officers, which he did.

Never once did he in any way seek to avoid the responsibilities of the South Yorkshire Police or himself. After the publication of the public inquiry report he offered his resignation to the police authority, which they declined. At every level he was strong, inspirational, compassionate, honourable and did everything he possibly could to help all those – not just police officers – hurt by what had occurred. He was the ultimate *paterfamilias*, holding the South Yorkshire police organisation together in a way that no one else could. I sincerely believe without doubt that he was the single most powerful unifying and healing factor of any in terms of restoring business continuity and normality, a man much admired within and without the police service for his professionalism and integrity.

That is the end of my story. I have attempted to give the reader an honest insight into the disaster experience from the inside. My concern is that the lessons learned at disasters often are not passed on and soon become forgotten and that this is unfortunate. It is to address that problem that I have made this contribution.

References

Sheffield *Star* (1994) Page one lead, 13 April

Taylor, L.J. (1989) *The Hillsborough Stadium Disaster 15 April 1989: Interim Report Cmd 765* London: HMSO

PART IV

LEARNING THE LESSONS

LEARNING THE LESSONS

Tredegar, South Wales, 2 December 1992: a coal tip collapses and covers the grounds of a comprehensive school. It seems that the lessons of Aberfan, a mere six miles away, have not been learned.

This final part of the book provides an opportunity to learn lessons from past crises and disasters, and from media coverage of them. In the process it looks in more detail at media liaison at disasters, including Dunblane, and at Exercise Malign Element, a training event set up to test plans and systems for dealing with a natural disaster.

Before considering these examples it is interesting to note that the rate of disasters world-wide continues to increase (Swiss Reinsurance 1989). The rate of socio-technical disasters, that is, those caused by human (often management) and technical failure combined, are increasing faster than the general trend (Keller 1989). This increase was reflected in the United Kingdom during the 1980s, the UK's worst disaster decade by far.

The cause of a disaster is rarely a simple matter to discover. While this is not the place to discuss this in detail, it seems clear that in recent times many problems are concerned with the increasing use of and reliance on information technology; the increasing rate of change in both the internal and external environments of many organisations; and straightforward failures of communication.

Furthermore, it is the experience of more than one of the contributors to this book that the changing nature of management responsibilities at times of crisis is often not understood by those involved.

There was a time when disasters were regarded as unforeseeable Acts of God. Inquiry chairmen would sometimes use that very phrase in their findings. The attention of those conducting inquiries, the media and the public tended to be on the disasters themselves and the aftermath, and not so much on the preparation or efforts made to prevent the occurrence.

Nowadays that has entirely changed. Executive and senior management often have a clear legal duty to anticipate these foreseeable events. They must make proper plans to avoid them and, when this is not possible, to minimise their impact when they occur. When those responsible do not do this and problems arise, then they will almost certainly be in breach of a duty of care to someone: clients, customers, staff, the general public or to whoever it is that they owe such a duty.

Thus there is a cast iron reason for learning the lessons and preparing to avoid crisis and disaster. If, however, disaster cannot be averted, organisations need to plan for how they will deal with the media's, the general public's, the investigating authorities' and the victims' needs for information. Good practice in prevention and preparation may mean the difference between the survival and the collapse of an organisation, and its reputation.

The two chapters which follow give practical advice on preparation. In the first Peter Whitbread draws on many years of experience in dealing with disasters and emergencies, and in running rehearsals and exercises. He counsels attention to detail and gives clear advice on the crucial points which will make the difference between a successful rehearsal and one which fails.

Chapter 14 brings together the lessons learned by press officers at a number of incidents to give advice about dealing with the media on the spot and in the immediate aftermath of disaster, when all around is chaos. Lessons on communication, the spokesperson role, delegation, the value of diversion and managing staff can be taken on board by most organisations.

Taken together with Mike Granatt's media handling strategies in Chapter 8 and Paddy Marley's check lists in Chapter 10, this part of the book forms a comprehensive guide to preparation and practice in communicating at a time of crisis, disaster or emergency.

References

Keller A. Z. (1989) 'The Bradford Scale' paper presented at Disaster Prevention and Limitation Conference, University of Bradford, 12–13 September

Swiss Reinsurance (1989) 'Sigma: Natural Catastrophes and Major Losses in 1988' *Economic Studies*: 1

13 TRAINING AND REHEARSAL

Peter Whitbread

Who is likely to be involved in a crisis, disaster or emergency? Most of the general public simply need information about the scale of the crisis, and reassurance that they are safe. Others, however, have roles which involve them in the maintenance of essential services, or of protecting and helping the public. Some will find themselves catapulted into a situation that calls for skills and qualities which have never previously been tested. Not only will they be called upon to draw on these reserves, but they will be required to do so at a time when they are under the microscope of huge public interest.

As society becomes more complex and fragmented, the number and diversity of those who may be called upon to help in a disaster increases. Fortunately it would be difficult to find another area of activity with the level of co-operation and support between individuals and organisations as exists in the area of emergency planning.

This should not come as a surprise. The whole ethos of protecting the public and community in the United Kingdom relies on a common understanding between the agencies and the individuals involved. Multi-agency co-operation has proved itself time and again in all parts of the country and at all levels in the community. In addition, co-operation with the media is vital in such situations, as the media are the main channel of communication with an organisation's various publics.

The basic principles of Integrated Emergency Management – risk assessment, accident prevention, emergency planning and incident response and recovery – demonstrate the need to raise awareness of the range of skills needed to mitigate the effects of the disaster.

Training and rehearsal will also lessen the effects of disaster. Lessons can be learned from those who have faced the worst, and through examination, debate and discussion the mistakes of the past can be avoided. The example in Exhibit 7 highlights the recent exercise Malign Element in which the Central Office of Information

(COI) were closely involved. The report illustrates how important exercises of this nature are.

Exercise Malign Element was a country wide exercise which took place in eastern England over the period 3–7 June 1996. Based on severe weather it was designed to accommodate exercising at a number of different levels to meet individual needs and collectively to contribute to an overall test of the country wide plans and systems. Handling the media was a major part of the exercise.

The COI featured in three roles. Virginia Burdon (COI regional director) played the role of news editor based at county headquarters; three members of staff played reporters in the field; and press enquiries were made by telephone by COI Eastern region staff. The following report was made at the end of the exercise, to enable those involved to look afresh at their training and resource needs

1 Media response

The media response was tested at a number of levels, with the pressure sustained by the introduction of 'leaks' of information to the press players and news room co-ordinators, to test response to *ad hoc* media pressure.

Press players and in the field press players reported that on occasion press officers did not seem to be adequately resourced to meet the demands that a real emergency would impose. They were also poorly briefed. Designated PROs sometimes appeared reluctant to deal with the press personally, detailing the task to more junior staff. Conversely, some spokespeople were confident and authoritative.

The response to telephone press enquiries was generally courteous but slack on essential detail. The personnel resources were barely adequate for the exercise purposes and a real emergency would require a much greater commitment. On occasion, media players were told that that spokespeople were 'too busy' to speak to them.

2 Scenario development

A recurring problem was the time lag between the injects of new information and delivery to the district at press officer level. Frequently press players were asking about developments which their timetable indicated had already taken place, but of which PROs were unaware because of delays in getting messages trafficked. The time lag varied between 15 and 45 minutes, raising serious doubts about communication systems. This is an issue that *must* be addressed if spokespeople are to be kept abreast of events and ahead of the media in a real emergency situation.

3 Spokespeople

The county chief executive performed effectively on television but was not put up to front a press conference during the exercise. The absence of a press conference was unrealistic since in a real emergency a conference or conferences at a county level would have been held with spokespeople from the various lead local authority departments participating.

4 Rumour and speculation

PROs responded nervously to injects which were fabricated or based on rumour and speculation. The county council itself tended to treat erroneous press reports as factual rather than confidently taking steps to remedy inaccurate coverage. There was no evidence of media monitoring at county council level other than taking a steer from media enquiries.

5 Contact with the Home Office

Contact with the lead central government department (Home Office) corporate communication team did not appear to have been carried out. News that a Home Office minister was visiting the region came from COI press players via the news editor, following confirmation that a media bid for an interview had been accepted.

6 News releases

These were highly variable in quality and presentation, with a tendency to be reactive.

7 Operation meetings

Were these minuted, and if so were minutes and advice on 'lines to take' forwarded electronically to a designated list, including district PROs?

Exhibit 7 Report on Exercise Malign Element
Source: COI

Common to any event will be skills which may be in demand in the normal course of events, such as medical skills, media relations, fire fighting abilities and so on. But the professional responding to an emergency may be called upon to exercise these skills in an environment which places extreme demands on them. For example, doctors and nurses could be placed in a situation where they are required to tend to victims of a bomb attack who are still lying trapped in the rubble of a building which is in danger of collapsing or being subjected to bombing.

Others have a responsibility for assessing risk as part of their normal responsibilities in their organisations such as welfare, safety or environmental legislation. Readers will readily remember how quickly the media alerted the general·public to scares such as the issue of salmonella in eggs, and the 'listeria hysteria', and how important it is to communicate effectively in the area of risk assessment and management.

The starting point in any emergency plan is an open-minded attitude. Training should encompass encouragement in spotting crisis indicators, and analysis of potential issues. Such issue tracking and analysis should be undertaken on a regular basis, with the team encouraged to think in terms of vulnerabilities, response strategies and contingency plans. One of the factors to guard against in tracking and analysis is a tendency to over-confidence – the 'it couldn't happen here' syndrome.

The organisational sociologist Charles Perrow's theory of the projected progress of errors and disturbances in many socio-technical systems propounds that they are not only inevitable but that they tend to compound and escalate in such a manner as to become unmanageable. Perrow identifies two crucial system properties: interactive complexity and tight coupling (Perrow 1984).

Interactive complexity is found in organisations such as chemical plants and mines, where two unconnected errors in such systems can interact in unforeseen ways. In tight coupling, processes happen very fast, cannot be turned off, and the failed parts cannot be isolated from other parts, or there is no other way to keep the production going safely. This compounds the problem and leads to its spreading 'quickly and irretrievably for at least some time'. Hence, a chemical plant is tightly coupled, whereas the mine is loosely coupled: an error or irregularity in the plant is liable to trigger a chain reaction which will lead to much greater devastation than an equivalent error in a mine. It has been argued that the theory can also be applied to social systems – a mass gathering of people in a relatively limited space can have similarly unpredictable susceptibilities (Parker and Handmer 1992).

The plan should involve a task force comprising people who are competent, able to make effective decisions and carry them out, as well as being specialists in areas which will be relevant to the crisis.

There should be a principal spokesperson whose job it is not only to communicate publicly on the crisis, but also to ensure that everyone involved in the crisis speaks with one voice.

Most failures in communication arise when insufficient consideration is taken of the needs of the various audiences, and advance consideration provides a basic understanding of how actions in dealing with one audience can indirectly affect others. The first 24 hours are crucial. It is at this time that the public's need for information is at its greatest and the information available is at its least. It is vital, however, that, even though not all of the information is available, that which is transmitted is accurate, consistent and up to date. It is also not enough simply to reassure without giving the facts. It is normal practice, for example, not to release victims' names until relatives have been informed. This does not, however, prevent the spokesperson from releasing the numbers involved – where known – or an estimate of the numbers when the exact total is not known.

Care must be of course, be exercised. Following the capsize of the *Herald of Free Enterprise*, the company was unaware of how many tickets had been sold for the voyage, and having calculated the number of deaths at 120, continued to quote that figure until the bodies were completely recovered five weeks later. The total number of fatal casualties was 193. The inaccuracy of the company's information was the source of much criticism of the company, and added distress to victims' families.

In addition, the plan should be co-ordinated with other potentially involved parties such as the local police, hospitals and others.

Clear lines of responsibility must be established, with provision for roles to change should a crisis arise. Internal struggles in the organisation introduce new difficulties and weaken its ability to deal effectively with the crisis.

Attention to detail is a guiding principle in developing any contingency plan. One of the criticisms levelled at the organisations dealing with the Zeebrugge and Lockerbie disasters was the inability of the public to get through on the phone to establish whether their relatives or friends were affected.

Although Pan Am had a crisis plan, the Lockerbie incident occurred following a period of downsizing in the corporation coupled with rapid advancements in the fields of technology and communications. The vice president of corporate communications at the company's headquarters quickly recognised the lack of staff and deficiencies in the telephone systems, but had no access to the extra resources needed to correct the problems. Relatives phoning the airline remember being greeted by taped Christmas carols, including an instrumental version of 'I'll be home for Christmas' (Deppa 1993).

Attention to detail is not the same thing as preparing a complex and detailed plan – too much detail is confusing and intimidating, and may obscure the priorities. In addition it will quickly become out of date. The plan should therefore be streamlined as much as possible.

However much responders prepare for a crisis, they will still need a re-briefing in the event of an actual crisis, and it is essential that copies of the plan are accessible to them.

A pre-determined crisis centre should be designated and equipped. To equip themselves to deal effectively with a disaster, responders can take advantage of training. Ideally they should also have access to rehearsal. The difference between the two is important; each fulfils different functions in terms of embedding the learning, and in addition, rehearsal serves to validate and inform the training process. The various types of training available include seminars, training days, open learning methods and media courses. There may even be opportunities to take on secondments or work shadowing, giving the opportunity for further professional development.

Anyone considering preparing themselves for a public role in an emergency would do well to start by making contact with the Home Office Emergency Planning College at Easingwold, York. The college runs a programme of short residential courses appropriate to a wide range of needs: fundamental, strategic, caring, technical or a more focused training need. If the college does not have a course for a particular training need, they are happy to discuss any special proposals. They can also arrange shadowing attachments.

In addition, the college library houses an extensive and unique collection of crisis, disaster and emergency planning related material in the form of books, videos, periodicals, slides, plans, reports and newspaper cuttings. It is the designated United Kingdom Documentation Centre for Emergency Planning of the European Commission, and access is freely available.

Private sector organisations take part in many of the courses held at the college. In addition most, if not all, major firms will have engaged the services of a public relations consultancy, or have an in-house PR department. Those who have not yet considered doing so should seriously assess the value of discussing their needs with a specialist crisis planning consultant.

As with all training, the potential emergency responder would be well advised to draw up a training needs analysis in the first instance. This should include the level of skill and knowledge required, the amount of time and budget available to commit to training and the time-scale in which the various competencies should be achieved. In addition, the analysis should indicate whether the type of training selected can help a delegate meet his or her continuing professional development needs.

Interview training is vital, to equip any potential spokespersons for dealing with the media. Journalists are expert professional interviewers, and any crisis will be the focus of concentrated media interest. The reporters on the scene will be under intense pressure to come up with a fresh angle and interesting stories about the event, and this is one of the most important elements of any crisis plan.

On completion of training, the newly equipped responder needs to practise his or her skills, and this is where rehearsal comes in. Rehearsal allows inexperienced people to role play and test out the application of their skills in a learning environment. The benefits of this are to allow the individual to build confidence, and to give the organisation an opportunity to test out its plans for dealing with a crisis. The importance and value of this should not be underestimated.

The Pan American Airways Boeing 747 *Maid of the Seas* took off from London Heathrow airport at 6.25 p.m. on 21 December 1988. It disappeared off the radar screen at 7.02.50. The first call logged at the regional fire control centre was timed at 7.04, and at approximately 7.05, journalists on the *Glasgow Herald* had been alerted. Scottish Television, and the BBC in London, estimated their information arrived at about the same time. By 7.30 the first bulletins were on the air, and the first reporters were on the scene within an hour. The fire which had resulted from the impact of the fuselage breaking through a section of gas main was not brought under control until four and a half hours after impact.

In the first hour of the disaster, communications were muddled — first intelligence suggested it was a military plane, then that the plane had crashed into a service station. Both the BBC and Scottish Television needed to ensure their calls were not a hoax, and needed information fast. In Britain, the families and friends of passengers on the plane were still driving home from waving them off, and in New York, families and friends were driving to the airport to collect passengers. Many of them heard about the crash first from the media. In addition, there were thousands more people who needed to be reassured that their families and friends were not on the plane which had crashed, and added to that, the need for the emergency services to deal effectively with the evacuation of Lockerbie survivors. It can be easily seen that anyone trying out their new-found skills in dealing with an emergency would be overwhelmed if they found themselves in this situation without any prior warning or support.

Fortunately, many of those officials involved on the ground at the Lockerbie disaster had received training in sophisticated media exposure. As well as equipping them with the skills to deal effectively with the world's media, the training had enabled them to function effectively together as a group.

It is true that people make elementary mistakes when confronted with a crisis, and may behave in ways which are not typical of their normal behaviour. The earliest stages of a crisis are the most crucial, because that is when the need for information is greatest, and the amount of information available is at its least. Preparation is the ultimate key.

The public must be kept fully informed at all times. Silence is not enough — without correct, consistent and up-to-date information, the vacuum will be filled with rumours and inaccuracies. An example of this was seen at Lockerbie, where a rumour took hold among families of victims from the United States that the personal property of their relatives would not be returned to them. Nothing could have been further from the truth, and nothing could have been more calculated to upset someone who had suffered a loss. The Pan Am team worked extremely hard at correcting this misinformation through the media, but they were unable to stem the flow of rumours. They eventually bypassed media channels altogether and contacted the victims' relatives directly to explain the true situation (Deppa *op. cit.*).

Rehearsal differs from actuality in several ways, of course. Firstly, respondents are warned that they will be participating in a rehearsal. Secondly there is no crisis, hence there will be no loss or threat of loss of life or injury, and there will be access to all normal facilities such as transport, communications, medical back-up and so on; thirdly, the rehearsal will be unlikely to attract the massive media attention that a real crisis will attract. By 1 a.m. on the night of the Lockerbie disaster it is estimated that 400 journalists had assembled at the scene, and that was just the start of intense media interest which lasted for months.

The Pan Am bombing over Lockerbie had a profound effect. It demonstrated how the way we deal with communication in the event of a disaster is changing because our ability to accumulate and communicate information has outstripped our capacity to understand the meaning of the messages the media transmit, and the impact of journalistic methods. An examination of the Lockerbie disaster will show that the factors which make a difference in performance are

- the existence of a formal crisis communication plan

- regular role playing by key officials of crisis scenarios

- the past experience of the principal communicators

- their level of understanding of journalistic practices in covering disasters

- a co-ordinated effort, with the ability to marshal forces and resources quickly and efficiently

- the presence, both real and symbolic, of the top person.

To construct a realistic rehearsal, it is useful to incorporate the following points (Parker and Handmer *op. cit.*)

1. the crisis scenario should seize the attention of its audience. By being dramatic, and emphasising potential dangers the rehearsal will help the responder to visualise disasters in a way which may not previously have been appreciated

2. the scenario must be accurate – based on scientific evidence and accurate predictions, analysed objectively

3. it must have legitimacy. In other words the rehearsal should involve those organisations which would be involved in reality

4. closely related to the above is the need for the rehearsal to be believable, that is, it may be accurate but so unlikely it fails to

draw the responder in. It may be useful to incorporate 'real-life' stories of victims, and 'key issues' for example to add realism to the scenario

5. one must be clear about the target audiences, and design the communication messages appropriately

6. there should be an outcome, with a proposed course of action, in the event of the scenario happening in actuality.

Within these parameters, the designer of the scenario should be alert to the contradictions and difficulties such scenarios present, and time spent in careful construction of the crisis scenario will be well spent. Rehearsal enables everyone to practise their role in advance, and allows the opportunity to identify further training needs and weaknesses in the plan. In addition to helping responders to prepare for their role in an emergency, rehearsals allow an opportunity to identify potential hazards, and feed this back in to the planning process.

It is also important when planning a major rehearsal to set a realistic time-scale and budget for the event. A recent county-wide exercise which involved a number of organisations was over a year in the planning stages, and cost £40,000. This exercise was considered by the organisers to be a day of mixed fortunes – not the complete success which had been hoped for, but not the complete disaster which had been feared.

Of the cost of the exercise, the event planning accounted for nearly 20 per cent of the total, and similar sums were expended on administration of the event and the expenses of outside organisations. More than 50 per cent of the total went on improvements to the communications systems, which were of continuing benefit to the organisations involved. Nevertheless, it is a significant sum, and in the present economic climate, difficult decisions may have to be made about an organisation's spending priorities.

There is no easy answer to this question, but as the examples quoted above demonstrate the costs of not carrying out such rehearsals can have grave consequences. In America, the Lockerbie disaster was a major factor in the eventual collapse of Pan American Airways. Following the sinking of *The Herald of Free Enterprise* at Zeebrugge, eight defendants were brought to trial on a charge of corporate manslaughter. Although in that instance, six defendants were acquitted, and the Crown withdrew its case against the remaining two, the principle of corporate responsibility appeared to be established.

Following a rehearsal, an evaluation is of course essential. This should be done by reference to the original aims and objectives of the rehearsal, and should incorporate feedback from all individuals and organisations involved. The feedback should cover strengths and weaknesses and ideas for improvement, and should obviously be as truthful and objective as possible. The lessons learned from the rehearsal can then be fed back into the planning process, and training needs analysed.

If the COI are used by the public sector as a player in rehearsal, COI press officers assigned to the disaster site would have been establishing links with the principal officers of the emergency services and with the press offices of the central government departments, local authorities and other organisations (e.g. hospitals) concerned – exchanging names, fax numbers and home and office telephone numbers in the process.

With these internal lines of communication sorted out a firm routine of press conferences and briefings would need to be established, in consultation with the media. Typically this might entail:

1. a pattern of regular press conferences in the press centre at, say, four-hourly intervals throughout the day and night, for the first 24 hours or so of the emergency. Each press conference would be in two parts: a progress report by, say, a senior police officer on operational aspects of the emergency (casualty figures, progress in restoring essential services, evacuation plans, and so on) followed by questions; and a briefing by government sources on the wider aspects (environmental and health implications, government funds for rehabilitation and repairs, possible public inquiry, and so on), followed by questions.

2. *ad hoc* briefings. In the early stages of the emergency one-to-one briefings would be discouraged – there would not be time for them and the media would probably accept this. But the set-piece press conferences might be augmented by *ad hoc* briefings on specific issues selected by the media (for example, a briefing on transport or safety issues by experts from the Department of Transport or the Health and Safety Executive). Similarly, the press

office might initiate special briefings of this kind if early media
reports revealed misconceptions on key issues.

3. photo facilities. The press office must keep in mind the needs of
    the visual media and would organise photo opportunities for
    television and stills photographers. In the early hours of an
    emergency these would need to be closely chaperoned; the
    presence of large numbers of photographers and television crews
    might otherwise hinder the work of the emergency services. As
    well as meeting media suggestions for news and picture facilities,
    the press office would itself be ready to propose facilities to help
    counter any unduly alarmist or exaggerated accounts of the
    incident that may have been circulated in its early stages. Subject
    to the numbers involved, there may be a need to establish some
    form of rota or pooling arrangement for all field facilities of this
    kind.

4. the regional angle. If the disaster affects a relatively small area –
    say a small town or village – the press office would need to make
    a point of meeting the special needs of the local and regional
    media (for example, for details of names and addresses of
    casualties, after next-of-kin had been informed) and of the effects
    on local services, school closures, road diversions and so on.

5. de-briefings. After each press conference or facility there would
    be a pattern of de-briefing sessions in the press office with
    members of the emergency services and with the principal
    spokespersons; to allocate follow-up tasks, to assess media
    coverage so far and to research and prepare question-and-answer
    briefs for the next press conference.

Implicit in all this is the recognition that the media have a vital
role to perform in civil emergencies. They are not mere extras in the
drama – to be tossed the odd scrap of news and then pushed away in
a corner. They have a right to be there, and a duty to perform while
they are there. As custodians of the public's right to know they
provide an essential channel – in a major disaster often the only
reliable channel – for conveying information, reassurance and advice
to the public at large – and to those immediately affected by the
disaster. Past experience has shown how responsibly they exercise
those rights and how thoroughly they perform those duties. None of
the known excesses of some of the tabloid media, in searching out

and exploiting the most harrowing aspects of a disaster, has diminished that high reputation overall.

Even so, press officers have to strike what can sometimes be a difficult balance. Obviously their primary objective is to assist the media to fulfil their role – but they cannot always give them everything they want. They must exercise a measure of control over the movements of the media, for example, if the presence of large numbers of media representatives is not to hinder the work of the emergency services. And there will be times when they will have to withhold – for legal or security reasons – information which the media knows exists and which they would desperately like to have for their next editions.

In short, press officers must both serve and control the demands of the media. Their success in performing the second of those functions is directly dependent on their success in performing the first. If the media have confidence in the efficiency and integrity of the press office, if they have been provided with reasonable access to the site and regular and authoritative briefings and updates on the steps that are being taken to deal with the emergency, they will be less inclined to produce speculative and misleading copy, or go out foraging off limits and get under the feet of the hard pressed emergency services.

This is a point worth making to those exasperated officials who from time to time might question the press officer's role in emergency situations and ask 'why are you paying all this attention to these media people?'

Part of the preparation for dealing with an emergency is to have a press kit. COI press officers are equipped with a kit which includes a COI-designed distribution amplifier linked to a microphone to give quality, clean sound feeds. It takes up to 15 connections for radio or television actuality, removing the need for a bank of microphones under the speaker's nose. It also includes a portable television set, video recorder, radio, cassette recorder, and a camera. In all, this provides a monitoring and recording service so the official on the spot knows what the national media are saying, and if necessary, can correct misinformation promptly.

Other equipment provided by COI includes a laptop computer, with modem connection to a cellphone, linked in to access overload or a land line. This can be used if the system is suddenly closed down to normal traffic because of pressure on the telephone network. Once the information reaches COI headquarters in London, the text of a message can be routed via COI's mailbox, the electronic news distribution service, or directly to the regional press. Then there are all the extras, intended to meet practical needs in what can be a chaotic situation: tabards and hard hats, torches, loud hailers and maps, right down to pens, presentational aids and a photocopier.

The addresses and phone numbers of the COI network are shown in Appendix 2 of this book.

The press kit for any organisation should include a press pack, which would be made available to representatives attending press conferences in the event of a crisis. The pack should include written background material about the incident, with the names and official titles of people who are involved, biographical information and other pertinent facts.

A standby statement can also be prepared in advance, setting out the policy which relates to any event that may develop into a crisis.

This chapter has briefly touched upon some of the issues to be considered in dealing with the media. This vital aspect of planning, training and rehearsal is also discussed as an issue in Chapter 2.

In any situation in which people find themselves dealing with a difficult situation, the qualities of foresight, confidence, maturity, level-headedness, good judgement, and reliability are valuable. In a crisis, disaster or emergency situation the value of such qualities is magnified. Put this together with training and experience and the organisation will have an excellent asset in that individual.

References

Deppa, J. (1993) *The Media and Disasters: Pan Am 103* London: David Fulton

Parker, D. and Handmer, J. (1992) *Hazard Management and Emergency Planning: Perspectives on Britain* London: James and James

Perrow, C. (1984) *Normal Accidents: Living with High-Risk Technologies* New York: Basic Books

14 MEDIA LIAISON: LESSONS FROM THE FRONT LINE

Shirley Harrison

In this chapter, which is based on the experiences of a number of press officers at major incidents, we will be drawing out some of the lessons learned about liaison with the media.

Communications

A major problem at incidents which attract large members of the media is that of communications between the different people and places. It is likely that the disaster site will be sealed off from the press at the earliest opportunity, especially if there is danger or if the location is a scene-of-crime. The press officer will then have the problem of where to be located – at the scene or with the media. Clearly a team of press officers is required so that both places can be covered, but there is still the problem of effective communication between the two. At one major shooting incident, the absence of any direct link to the senior investigation officer via land telephone lines, cellnet telephones or personal radio meant that effective communication could only be maintained by personal visits to the site of the incident. This in turn had a serious effect on the speed with which the press team could respond to media enquiries with accurate information, leaving the media to resort to speculation.

The press team in such a situation needs to be equipped with effective means of communicating with the senior investigating officer or incident commander. It is also important to ensure that effective communication is achieved and maintained between all staff in the press office. The pressure of enquiries and requests for interviews is often so great that communication simply breaks down. Members of staff need to be regularly updated with new information as it is released from the senior investigating officer.

In addition communication between the coroner's office, hospitals and so on needs to be clear and continuous. Lack of communication in this important area can result in the identities of dead and injured people being released to the media prior to completion of the formal identification process at the mortuary. Having a press officer in attendance at the mortuary, or at least diverting calls and enquiries to the press office, where checking can take place, can ensure this very distressing scenario does not happen.

Spokesperson

At any major incident or investigation the media always prefer to have access to the senior investigating officer or incident commander and they will not normally settle for access to the press officer only. There can be exceptions, for example when it is plain that the disaster is of such a scale that the senior person has to remain at the site and is simply too busy concentrating on the task in hand to give interviews.

Where this happens, the media will usually be willing to accept a spokesperson, as long as it is made clear that this person is speaking with the authority of the senior officer in charge, and is, so to speak, relaying that officer's comments. Another issue arises here as to the credibility of someone speaking on behalf of a senior police officer: does that person – the official police spokesperson – have the same credibility if they are out of uniform? Certainly there is a question here about whether or not senior police officers, rather than civilians, should be in charge of police press offices. This is perhaps an area that is worthy of further discussion and consideration by police forces which have set up or are in the process of setting up press offices.

Delegation

The lesson learned from a number of incidents is quite simply not to try to do everything yourself but to delegate as much as possible to other members of the press team. In a major incident it is neither feasible nor desirable for one person to try and deal with all media liaison, although of course it is vital that one person is in charge of co-ordination.

For press offices where only one person is employed on media liaison, here is an issue of forward planning. While on cannot staff up for the disaster that may never happen, some sort of contingency arrangement must be made so that a one-person-band does not have to try and deal with everything on the day. Large organisations could agree in advance to share or loan their press officers to neighbouring smaller organisations in the event of a major disaster, for example.

Equipment

The press office, like every other function at a major incident, must have access to proper equipment. That equipment should include

- properly marked yellow reflective jackets
- cellnet telephones
- personal radios
- stand alone word processors
- television sets and recording equipment
- flip charts
- clip-boards
- stationery
- a fax machine
- a photocopier
- sufficient land telephone lines
- a PA system
- portable Mercury newslink (giving access to every news agency in the country)
- a dedicated vehicle

In addition the police force's contingency plan should make clear the procedures to be adopted by the press office in relation to the setting up of an appropriate press centre and the establishment of media holding areas and rendezvous points at or near to the site of the incident.

Value of diversion

At the scene of a disaster which may also be the scene of a crime, the press office will be confronted with a situation where, apart from confirming details of what has actually happened at the incident, no other information can be provided to the media, as future judicial proceedings have rendered the whole matter *sub judice*. Hundreds of reporters and photographers will thus have to be provided with alternative story lines in an attempt to divert them away from the families involved and to prevent damaging investigative journalism.

Journalists have a saying that if you 'feed the beast then the beast will remain contented and will not become troublesome. If you fail to feed the beast then the beast will go looking for food and that is when problems will arise'. As we have seen in the earlier chapters on Hillsborough, it is possible to feed the beast by providing access to those who are involved, if indirectly, and who wish to speak to the media. Press conferences can be set up with representatives from appropriate authorities or departments, independent experts and advisers (say from a local university department) and a representative from a similar organisation or group from elsewhere.

In addition photo opportunities can be organised, for example at the display of flowers which will almost certainly materialise following a disaster. The press officer needs to put him or herself in the position of the reporter or photographer, and think what would make a good story or picture, and then provide it. Heart-warming stories of human interest can help to counteract more damaging stories and act as an antidote to depressing or perhaps disturbing news from elsewhere.

Press accreditation

Press centres at a disaster appear to attract a fair proportion of cranks, sight-seers and hangers-on. It is important to control access using some kind of press accreditation to ensure that only bona fide members of the media have access to the press centre. This, again, is something that should be considered before the disaster occurs, so that a simple arrangement is ready to go on the day, with the minimum of fuss. Anything complicated will not work.

Pool arrangements

Pool arrangements for press access can work well, or can be problematic. Clive Ferguson's advice in Chapter 3 to allow the media to sort themselves out is sound, as getting involved in squabbles between warring journalists is counter-productive.

However, the way in which pooling is approached with the media *is* important. Journalists have to know that there is a good reason for it before they will, albeit grudgingly, agree. Administrative convenience or not enough chairs are not good reasons. If all else fails, strong policing of the pool may be the only alternative. In one incident the involvement of the Scottish National Newspaper Society had to be sought to act as independent arbiters in the selection of journalists for the pool.

Liaison with press officers from other agencies involved

All other agencies involved at the scene of a disaster must be made aware that one press officer, and one only, is the official spokesperson on the incident. In the early stages, that person will almost always be the police press officer. He or she alone is authorised to make statements about the incident to the media and nobody else, not medical authorities, nor the ambulance service, should do so. Statements about matters such as the numbers of persons injured and the types of injuries involved could result in inaccurate information getting into the hands of the relatives via the media. It could even jeopardise the outcome of any future criminal proceedings or indeed influence the findings of a fatal accident inquiry or public inquiry.

Staff rotation

It is a feature of disasters that, once the staff for the press office are in place, they are most reluctant to take rest periods or indeed be relieved at any time by fresh staff. To make them go home at such a time can prove counter productive and have an adverse effect on their morale. Indeed, there are advantages in the same staff working all the time, in that there are no hand-over problems and continuity can be maintained.

However, no-one can work at full stretch for a prolonged period, especially when the work they are engaged in is distressing in itself. Some staff rotation must occur and it must be handled sensitively.

It is important to develop the skills that enable the senior manager to identify those who need to take a break, and make sure they get one. It is equally important to be able to spot those who are not able to cope with the stresses and strains of the incident itself.

Such staff may need to be taken off the incident and assigned to other duties, and while this must be done with sensitivity, it must also be done promptly and firmly.

Trauma counselling

In many previous incidents, counselling was not available to those who had worked in the aftermath of disaster. However, it is now common practice for counselling to be offered, and in some cases insisted upon by employing organisations.

Sometimes the physical distance between the press centre and the scene of the disaster seems to detach press officers from the reality of the situation – but not from the pressures generated. This can lead to frustration, and a resulting inappropriate response. This problem may be addressed by taking press officers in ones and twos to visit the incident site to see for themselves the bullet holes or the rubble or the burned-out buildings, and the flower tributes and messages from around the world.

15 POSTSCRIPT

Shirley Harrison

At about 9.40 on the morning of 13 March 1996 an armed man, Thomas Hamilton, entered Dunblane Primary School. He shot dead 16 children and their class teacher, and then shot himself. Within a few minutes reports of the shooting were being given on television and within the hour every radio and television station was broadcasting the story. The small town of Dunblane came under immediate media siege.

On Saturday 16 March, the following urgent message was wired to all news editors.

URGENT NOTE TO NEWS EDITORS – DUNBLANE

The following statement has been issued today, Saturday 16th March 1996, by Superintendent Louis Munn, force press officer, Strathclyde Police, who is working in conjunction with Central Scotland Police following recent events in Dunblane. 'The media facility being offered this afternoon with families of the victims is an attempt to halt press intrusion into the lives of all the victims. I am now being informed personally by families that this intrusion is continuing unabated. Please be advised that if contact with the victims' families does not stop forthwith, I will take the matter up personally at the highest levels. The families have been told to pass the names of reporters and the organisations who continue to invade their privacy to me personally'.

The following Monday the *Guardian* ran a feature article by Jon Snow, presenter of *Channel 4 News*, discussing the role of the media at a time of crisis, disaster or tragedy (Snow 1996). He looked at the ways in which the different media covered the story: whether television cameras went for a wide or narrow lens, the use of the class

photograph and pictures of Thomas Hamilton, the extent to which
Dunblane was a 'news event' or an unbearable tragedy. As we have
seen elsewhere, that distinction is made by distance. The reporters on
the ground in Dunblane were deeply affected by the event they were
covering and many could not wait to leave (IPI 1996). On the other
hand the news managers, many of them hundreds of miles away, were
keen to get the best coverage.

Some of these media managers were quoted at the end of Snow's
article. Fred Bridgland, assistant editor in charge of news at the
Scotsman, the major national newspaper in Scotland, said that the
paper's priority was to respect the feelings of the people of Dunblane.

> We therefore put the emphasis on quality reporting and
> restraint … we banned sensationalist and cliched language,
> for example phrases like 'the slaughter of the innocents'.
> This restraint also applied to pictures. We didn't run the
> class group photo on our front page because it is an
> upsetting image and may have caused offence in Dunblane.
> Instead we used a picture of a woman weeping in the arms
> of a policewoman, neither of their faces visible.

This echoes Alf Green's decision, reported in Chapter 9, to
illustrate the Hillsborough disaster with a carefully cropped picture of
a tearful survivor rather than with pictures of the victims.

The *Guardian*, in common with most of the London based
papers, did use the class photograph. But the deputy editor (news),
Paul Johnson, felt they did so with proper respect and dignity.

> I believe it was quite right for the Guardian to use the class
> photo on our Thursday front page. That told us more than
> any other image, any other quote. But the following day's
> use by some papers of that picture with labels saying 'died'
> or 'injured' was crude and offensive. As was the *Independent*'s
> front page on Friday, showing Hamilton in a gym with three
> young boys stripped to the waist.

Fred Bridgland found the *Independent*'s front page

very distasteful. If we [the *Scotsman*] ran anything like that our readership would be rightly horrified.

Stuart Higgins, the editor of Britain's largest circulation tabloid, the *Sun*, acknowledged that

there is a sensational side to the coverage because it's the most remarkable story ever. I can't recall anything like it.

John Allen, executive editor of BBC radio news, echoed this view of Dunblane as a one-off in news terms, but made a telling point about learning lessons from the past; in this case from the shootings in Hungerford, another small, rural town.

It's the most difficult story Radio 5 Live has had to cover, and we have all been searching for a style and tone very rarely used. We've all discovered through going back to Hungerford to see how a town recovers, that the people see the press as half the problem because they associate media coverage with the tragedy. For this reason we started pulling people out of Dunblane on Friday.

The comments reported above illustrate a natural enough attempt by media managers to justify the way in which they covered Dunblane. Yet protestations of taste and sensitivity aside, every reporter wants to be first with the story or, if they cannot, to get a different angle on the story. The perceived custodians of the story – the director of the company to which the crisis or disaster has happened, the police officer investigating the incident, the grieving relative who won't hand over a photograph of the victim – all get in the way of the reporter. It is unsurprising that sides are taken and hostilities break out.

The Media Emergency Forum is an attempt to generate discussion about the seemingly irreconcilable needs of the different parties. Set up in the wake of a report by the Educational Broadcasting Trust it brings together journalists, editors and media managers; members of the emergency services and local authorities; and representatives of companies in such fields as transport and the nuclear industry. The forum has allowed members to talk about difficulties they have caused each other in the past, which have led to distrust on both sides: journalists believe that officialdom and businesses never tell the truth, while the latter believe that reporters distort the facts and get in the way. They have discussed – and rejected – a number of practical suggestions for dealing with reporting of disasters and emergencies, such as the creation of a roving 'media disaster squad' of press officers who would attend every event. More acceptable to forum members is the model of Norfolk's Pivot Centre, which receives and co-ordinates information from the emergency services' press officers, relaying it to an off-site bureau run by the police, and with media facilities (*Civil Protection* 1997b). It is hoped that the forum will go some way to helping the media, those responsible for media liaison, and organisations involved in crises and disasters to understand each other better.

Better understanding does not mean a too-cosy relationship. But it should lead to a climate of trust. It is imperative that the press maintain its questioning and investigative role, but how its members conduct themselves when doing their job is an issue. As an example, the behaviour of the press and their alleged part in the accident which caused the death of the Princess of Wales in 1997 caused an immense public outcry all over the world. This led in Britain to a re-think by the Press Complaints Commission on the whole issue of privacy and intrusion.

On the other hand, while organisations and individuals rightly seek to protect their reputation, there are examples of companies which have lied through their teeth in order to protect profits. The A. H. Robins company, makers of the Dalkon Shield birth control device, ignored evidence of massive bleeding, pelvic inflammatory diseases, miscarriages and deaths, publicly proclaiming that the product was safe (Hartley 1991). The history of crises, disasters and emergencies is populated by company spokespeople, press officers and political spin doctors who have gone out of their way to evade or obscure the reporting of detrimental information by the media. They all run the risk of being found out, which in Robins' case led to this verdict from the judge who presided over the compensation case

> You have taken the bottom line as your guiding beacon and the low road your route. (Lord 1984)

The key to unlock this problem is not found in check lists, manuals of good practice or complex rehearsals and exercises, invaluable though these are. The over-riding principle is integrity. If all parties involved in a crisis, disaster or emergency act and speak with integrity, it is clear that they have nothing to hide. Thus respect for each other's professional position, and hence an enhancement of their relationship, can be achieved.

References

Civil Protection (1997b) 'Disaster coverage: reporters and incident managers finally talk' in *Civil Protection* number 42 London: Home Office

IPI (1996) *Dunblane: reflecting tragedy* London: British Executive of the International Press Institute

Hartley, R. (1991) *Management Mistakes and Successes* 3rd edition New York: Wiley

Lord, Federal District Judge M. (1984) quoted in 'A Plea for Corporate Conscience' *Harpers* June

Snow, J. (1996) 'What should the message be?' London: *The Guardian* 18 March

APPENDIX 1

The Emergency Planning College

The Home Office Emergency Planning College exists to promote a heightened awareness of good practice in emergency preparedness. It does this through a programme of residential seminars and workshops held at The Hawkhills, a country house on the outskirts of Easingwold near York. The programme is run by specialists, and utilises full-time staff tutors as well as recognised experts, who are invited to contribute as visiting speakers.

The programme of seminars and workshops includes events for a number of different groups, generalist and specialist. These include managers in the private and public sectors: those working in retailing, the chemical industry, transport, the health service and the telecommunications business; civil servants; emergency planners; local authority chief executives; voluntary organisations; people who run sports grounds, pop concert venues and other stadia; elected members of local councils and those concerned with the safety and welfare of the general public. Most relevant to readers of this book are the following courses.

News Media and Information seminar, a three-day event which is open to public and private sector participants and which runs four or five times a year. Its aim is to examine relations between the news media and those with a public information role at a time of disaster, and to promote good practice. Most of the contributors to this book have at some time contributed to this seminar.

Emergency Management seminar, a three-day event aimed at senior managers with corporate organisational responsibilities. It has been developed to raise awareness of the strategic issues involved in managing a major crisis, including the examination of the discharge of corporate responsibilities, and the benefits of good media relations.

Inter-Departmental Plans workshop, which allows teams from local authorities to devise their own template for an emergency plan. Restricted to 25 delegates, the workshop ensures that every participant receives intensive practical training over the three days of the event.

215

Metropolitan and Urban Area Authorities seminar, also aimed at the public sector, and designed for local government, emergency services and voluntary organisations. The core of the event is an exercise which puts delegates under pressure as the scenario of a major incident unfolds before them. It provides the opportunity to learn about and practice planning and communicating in a crisis, as well as learning lessons from past incidents.

Subjects covered in other workshops and seminars, ranging from a day to a week in length, include Local Government Senior Management, Hazardous Materials and Pollution, Crowd Related Emergencies, Disaster and the Built Environment, Safety at Entertainment and Sports Venues, Dealing with Major Incidents, Understanding Radiation, Risk Assessment and Rest Centre Management.

The college also houses an extensive library and information centre, the UK's designated centre for emergency planning information. In addition to its collection of books, articles and reports the library subscribes to over 70 journals, including those concerned with emergency planning. It also has a selection of emergency plans, a collection of reports on exercises undertaken, over 22,000 newspaper cuttings and over 300 videos. Library stock is available to delegates attending courses at the college during their time there, and also for loan afterwards. It also serves those with an interest in emergency planning, crises and disasters who are not at the college. Those wishing to pursue a particular research angle can book library time on an individual basis.

The Home Office Emergency Planning College
The Hawkhills
Easingwold
York
YO6 3EG

Telephone 01347 821406

APPENDIX 2

The Central Office of Information (COI) network

Eastern
Three Crowns House, 72–80 Hills Road, Cambridge, CB2 1LL
Tel: 01223 311867 Fax: 01223 316121
Covers: Bedfordshire, Cambridge, Essex, Hertfordshire, Norfolk and Suffolk

Midlands East
Belgrave Centre, Level C, Stanley Place, Talbot Street, Nottingham, NG1 5GG
Tel: 0115 9712780 Fax: 0115 9712791
Covers: Derbyshire (except High Peak), Leicestershire, Lincolnshire, Nottinghamshire and Northamptonshire

Midlands West
Five Ways House, Islington Row, Middleway, Edgbaston, Birmingham, B15 1SH
Tel: 0121 626 2028 Fax: 0121 626 2041
Covers: Hereford and Worcester, Shropshire, Staffordshire, Warwickshire and West Midlands

North East
Wellbar House, Gallowgate, Newcastle upon Tyne, NE1 4TB
Tel: 0191 201 3300 Fax: 0191 261 8571
Covers: Cleveland, Durham, Northumberland, Tyne and Wear

North West
Sunley Tower, Piccadilly Plaza, Manchester, M1 4BD
Tel: 0161 952 4500 Fax: 0161 236 9443
Covers: Cheshire, Cumbria, Greater Manchester, High Peak District, Lancashire and Merseyside

South East
Hercules Road, London, SE1 7DU
Tel: 0171 261 8795 Fax: 0171 928 6974
Covers: Berkshire, Buckinghamshire, East Sussex, Greater London,
Hampshire, Isle of Wight, Kent, Oxfordshire, Surrey and West Sussex

South West
The Pithay, Bristol, BS1 2NF
Tel: 0117 9273767 Fax: 0117 9298612
Covers: Avon, Cornwall (including the Isles of Scilly), Devon, Dorset,
Gloucestershire, Somerset and Wiltshire

Yorkshire and Humberside
City House, New Station Street, Leeds, LS1 4JG
Tel: 0113 2836591 Fax: 0113 2836586
Covers: Humberside, North Yorkshire, South Yorkshire and West
Yorkshire

REFERENCES

Auf der Heide, E. (1989) *Disaster Response: Principles of Preparation and Co-ordination* Baltimore: C. V. Mosby

BBC (1993) *Producers' Guidelines* London: British Broadcasting Corporation

Bell, M. (1997) 'Here is the war, live by satellite' London: *Guardian* 8 March. See also *British Journalism Review* March 1997

Berge, D. ten (1988) *The First 24 hours: A Comprehensive Guide to Successful Crisis Communications* Oxford: Blackwell

Bradford Council (1986) *Out of the Valley: Bradford MDC's response to the Bradford City Fire Disaster 1985–1986* Bradford: Policy Unit

Buckingham, L. (1997) 'Dead customers do not have to hurt share price' *Guardian* 1 March

Casswell, T. (1996) 'The Hillsborough Report: a summary in pictures' in *Journeys of Discovery: Creative Learning from Disaster* London: National Institute for Social Work

Chippindale, P. and Horrie, C. (1990) *Stick it up Your Punter: the rise and fall of the Sun* London: Heinemann

Civil Protection (1997a) 'Plans to ease double trauma' 43 London: Home Office

Civil Protection (1997b) 'Disaster coverage: reporters and incident managers finally talk' 42 London: Home Office

Davies Sir H. E. (1967) *Tribunal Appointed to Inquire into the Disaster at Aberfan on October 21st 1966 Report HL316 and HC 553* London: HMSO

Deppa, J. (1993) *The Media and Disasters: Pan Am 103* London: David Fulton

Fennell, D. (1988) *Investigation into the King's Cross Underground Fire Cmd 499* London: HMSO

Fursland, E. (1996) 'Still Gagging on the Truth' London: *Guardian* 20 July

Harrison, S. (1997) 'Earning trust by telling the truth: how should public relations and media professionals behave when a disaster happens?' *Journal of Communication Management* 1 (3)

Hartley, R. (1991) *Management Mistakes and Successes* 3rd edition New York: Wiley

Home Office (1997) *Dealing with Disaster* 3rd edition Liverpool: Brodie

IPI (1996) *Dunblane: Reflecting Tragedy* London: British Executive of the International Press Institute

Ingham, B. (1994) Comment column London: *Daily Express* 30 June

Keller A. Z. (1989) 'The Bradford Scale' Paper presented at Disaster Prevention and Limitation Conference, University of Bradford, 12–13 September

Liverpool *Echo* (1997) 'Doctor's crucial new evidence' Liverpool: 26 February

Newburn, T. (1996) 'Some Lessons from Hillsborough' in *Journeys of Discovery: Creative Learning from Disaster* London: National Institute for Social Work

Parker, D. and Handmer, J. (1992) *Hazard Management and Emergency Planning: Perspectives on Britain* London: James & James

Perrow, C. (1984) *Normal Accidents: Living with High-Risk Technologies* New York: Basic Books

Scraton, P., Jemphrey, A. and Coleman, S. (1995) *No Last Rights: The Denial of Justice and the Promotion of Myth in the Aftermath of the Hillsborough Disaster* Liverpool: Liverpool City Council Hillsborough Project

Shearer, A. (1991) *Survivors and the Media* London: John Libbey

Snow, J. (1996) 'What should the message be?' London: *Guardian* 18 March

The Star (1989) Page one lead, Sheffield: 22 April

The Star (1994) Page one lead, Sheffield: 13 April

Sunday Times (1993) London: 28 February

Swiss Reinsurance (1989) 'Sigma: Natural Catastrophes and Major Losses in 1988' *Economic Studies:* 1

Taylor, L.J. (1989) *The Hillsborough Stadium Disaster 15 April 1989: Interim Report Cmd 765* London: HMSO

UNDHA (1995) *UNDHA News:* 14

FURTHER READING

Part I

Algar, P. (1992) *Managing Industrial Emergencies: a planning and communications guide* (Financial Times Management Report) London: Financial Times Business Information

Barton, L. (1993) *Crisis in Organizations: managing and communicating in the heat of chaos* Cincinnati, Ohio: South Western Publishing

Bernstein, D. (1988) *Company Image and Reality* London: Cassell

Bland, M. (1995) 'Strategic Crisis Management' in N. Hart (ed.) *Strategic Public Relations* Basingstoke: Macmillan

Charles, M. and Kim, J. (1988) *Crisis Management: a casebook* New York NY: C. C. Thomas

Darling, J. (1994) 'Crisis Management in International Business' *Leadership & Organization Development Journal* 15 (8)

Dowling, G. (1994) *Corporate Reputations* London: Kogan Page

Emergency Planning College (1994) *Crises in a Complex Society* Easingwold Papers (7) Easingwold: Home Office Emergency Planning College

Fink, S. (1986) 'Crisis Forecasting: what's the worst that could happen?' *Management Review* 53 (7)

Fitzpatrick, K. (1993) 'Who's in Charge: Balancing Public Relations and Legal Counsel in a Crisis' *Journal of Corporate Public Relations* Winter

Gottschalk, J. (ed.) (1993) *Crisis Response: inside stories on managing image under siege* Washington, DC: Visible Ink

Grunig, J. and Hunt, T. (1984) *Managing Public Relations* Orlando: Holt, Rinehart & Winston

Harrison, S. (1995) *Public Relations: an introduction* London: Routledge/International Thomson Business Press

Hart, N. (Ed.) (1995) *Strategic Public Relations* Basingstoke: Macmillan

Haywood, R. (1994) *Managing Your Reputation* London: McGraw Hill

Jowett, G. and O'Donnell, V. (1992) *Propaganda and Persuasion* 2nd edition London: Sage

Kitchen, P. (Ed.) (1997) *Public Relations Principles and Practice* London: International Thomson Business Press

Lagadec, P. (1990) *States of Emergency* Oxford: Butterworth Heinemann

McGregor, I. (1997) 'The public inquiry maze' *Civil Protection* 42 London: Home Office

Meyers, G. with Holuhsa, J. (1986) *When It Hits the Fan: Managing the Nine Crises of Business* Boston, Mass.: Houghton Mifflin

Mintzberg, H. (1987) 'The Strategy Concept II: another look at why organizations need strategies' *California Management Review* Fall

Mitroff, I. and Pauchant, T. (1990) *We're So Big and Powerful Nothing Bad Can Happen to Us* New York: Carol

Mitroff, I. (1986) 'Teaching corporate America to think about crisis prevention' *Journal of Business Strategy* 6

Picton-Phillipps, T. (1996) 'Corporate Killing' *Civil Protection* 39 London: Home Office

Pinsdorf, M. (1987 *Communicating When Your Company is Under Siege* Lexington, Mass.: Lexington Books

Quarantelli, E. (1988) 'Disaster Crisis Management: a summary of research findings' *Journal of Management Studies* July: 373–385

Regester, M. (1990) *Crisis Management: what to do when the unthinkable happens* London: Hutchinson

Richardson, B. (1995) 'Paradox Management for Crisis Avoidance' *Management Decision* 33 (1) 5–18

Smith, D. (1990) 'Beyond contingency planning: towards a model of crisis management' *Industrial Crisis Quarterly* 4 (4)

Stone, N. (1995) *The Management and Practice of Public Relations* Basingstoke: Macmillan

Toft, B. and Reynolds, S. (1994) *Learning from Disasters: a management approach* Oxford: Butterworth Heinemann

Walsh, M. (1989) *Disasters: Current Planning and Recent Experience* London: Hodder and Stoughton

Part II

Bentall, J. (1993) *Disasters, Relief and the Media* London: Tauris

Boyd, A. (1994) *Broadcast Journalism* Oxford: Focal Press

Cate, F. (1994) 'Harnessing the power of communications to avert disasters and save lives' *Report* Washington, DC: Northwestern University Communications Policy Studies

Cavalier, R. (1993) 'Disaster and the Media' *Macedon Digest* Winter

Civil Protection (1993) 'The CNN Factor: disaster communications and the media' 29 London: Home Office

Cumberbatch, G. and Howitt, D. (1989) *A Measure of Uncertainty: the effects of the mass media* London: John Libbey

Emergency Planning College (1991) *Seminar Report on Crises and the Media* Easingwold Papers (2) Easingwold: Home Office Emergency Planning College

Davey, N. (1996) 'The Manchester Bomb' *Civil Protection* 40 London: Home Office

Downing, J., Mohammadi, A. and Sreberny, A. (eds.) (1995) *Questioning the Media: A Critical Introduction* London: Sage

Franklin, B. and Murphy, D. (in press) *Making the News: Local Newspapers, Local Media and Local Journalism* London: Routledge

Harris, G. and Spark, D. (1993) *Practical Newspaper Reporting* Oxford: Focal Press

Home Office (1997) *Dealing with Disaster* 3rd edition, Liverpool: Brodie

Irvine, R. (1987) *When You Are the Headline: managing a major news story* Homewood, Ill.: Dow-Jones Irwin

Keeble, R. (1994) *The Newspapers Handbook* London: Routledge

Kelly, A., Gibson, R. and Horlick-Jones, T. (1992) 'Local Authorities, the Media, and Disasters: developing a peacetime emergency media strategy' *Report* London: Emergency Planning Information Centre (EPICENTRE)

Keys, C. (1993) 'Uneasy bedfellows: emergency managers and the media' *Macedon Digest* Winter

McNair, B. (1996) *News and Journalism in the UK* 2nd edition, London: Routledge

National Academy of Sciences (1980) *Disasters and the Mass Media* Washington DC: NAS

Nohrstedt, S. (1993) 'Communicative Action in the Risk Society: Public Relations Strategies, the Media and Nuclear Power' in A. Hansen, (ed.) *The Mass Media and Environmental Issues* Leicester University Press

Partington, A. and Savage, P. (1985) 'Disaster Planning: managing the media' *British Medical Journal* 291 (31 August)

Ploughman, P. (1997) 'Disasters, the Media and Social Structures: A typology of credibility hierarchy persistence based on newspaper coverage of the Love Canal and six other disasters' *Disasters* 21 (2)

Quarantelli, E. (1988) 'Disaster Crisis Management: a summary of research findings' *Journal of Management Studies* 25

Scanlon, T., Alldred, S., Farrell, A. and Prawzick, A. (1985) 'Coping with the Media in Disasters: some predictable problems' *Public Administration Review Special Issue*

Singer, B. and Green L. (1972) *The Social Functions of Radio in a Community Emergency* Toronto: Copp Clark Publishing

Smeeton, C. (1995) 'Local government news' *Civil Protection* 36 London: Home Office [Knight Air crash]

Smith, C. (1992) *Media and Apocalypse* Greenwood: London

Taylor, S. (1992) *Shock! Horror! The tabloids in action* London: Black Swan

United Nations High Commission for Refugees *Reports of the UN Commission on Human Rights In Iraq (E/CN.4/1993/45)*: Special Rapporteur Max van der Stoel: Geneva: UNHCR

Wallbaum, D. (1994) 'How will your company handle the press and disasters?' *Disaster Recovery* Summer

Walters, L., Wilkins, L. and Walters, T. (eds.) (1989) *Bad Tidings: Communication and catastrophe* London: Lawrence Erlbaum

Wenger, D. and Friedman, B. (1986) 'Local and National Media Coverage of Disaster: a content analysis of the print media's treatment of disaster myths' *International Journal of Mass Emergencies and Disasters* 4

White, D. (1991) 'A Media Reflection on Disaster' *Macedon Digest* Summer

Williams, G. (1996) *Britain's Media: How they are related* 2nd edition, London: Campaign for Press and Broadcasting Freedom

Williams, P. and Conroy, A. (1994) *The Radio Handbook* London: Routledge

Wilkins, L. and Patterson, P. (1987) 'Risk analysis and the construction of news' *Journal of Communication* 37

Yorke, I. (1995) *Television News* 3rd edition Oxford: Focal Press

Part III

Coleman, S., Jemphrey, A., Scraton, P. and Skidmore, P. (1990) *Hillsborough and After: the Liverpool Experience* Liverpool: Liverpool City Council Hillsborough Project

Elliott, D. and Smith, D. (1993) 'Football stadia disasters in the United Kingdom: learning from tragedy' *Industrial and Environmental Crisis Quarterly* 7 (3) 205–229

Jacobs, B. and Hart, P. (1992) 'Disaster at Hillsborough Stadium: a comparative analysis' in D. Parker and J. Handmer *Hazard Management and Emergency Planning: Perspectives on Britain* London: James & James

Kervern, G. (1993) 'Studying Risks: the Science of Cindynics' *Business Ethics* 2 (3) 140–2

Newburn, T. (1993) *Making a Difference? Social Work After Hillsborough* London: National Institute for Social Work

Newburn, T. (1993) 'Some Lessons from Hillsborough' *Civil Protection* 27 London: Home Office

Press Council (1989) 'The Hillsborough Inquiry: Press coverage of the disaster at Hillsborough Stadium, Sheffield on 15 April 1989' *Report No. 1* London: Press Council

Richardson, W. (1993) 'Identifying the cultural causes of disasters: an analysis of the Hillsborough football stadium disaster' *Journal of Contingencies and Crisis Management* 1 (1)

Shapiro, D. and Kunkler, J. (1990) 'Psychological Support for Hospital Staff Initiated by Clinical Psychologists in the Aftermath of the Hillsborough Disaster' *Report* Sheffield: Trent RHA

Taylor, L.J. (1990) *The Hillsborough Stadium Disaster 15 April 1989: Final Report Cmd 962* London: HMSO

Trent Regional Health Authority/Merseyside Regional Health Authority (1990) 'Hillsborough: the lessons for health care' *Report* Sheffield: Trent RHA

Wardrope, J. *et al.* (1991) 'The Hillsborough Tragedy' *British Medical Journal* 303 (30 November)

Williams, J. and Wagg, S. (eds.) (1991) *British Football and Social Change: Getting into Europe* Leicester University Press

Part IV

Allinson, R. (1993) *Global Disasters: Inquiries into Management Ethics* New York: Simon & Schuster

Bivins, T. (1993) 'Public Relations, Professionalism and the Public Interest' *Journal of Business Ethics* 12

Civil Protection (1996) 'Exercise puts Essex to the test' 40 London: Home Office

Clutterbuck, D., Dearlove, D. and Snow, D. (1992) *Actions Speak Louder: a management guide to corporate social responsibility* London: Kogan Page

Davis, K. (1967) 'Understanding the social responsibility puzzle' *Business Horizons* Winter

Escott, S. (1997) 'Exercise media plans' *Civil Protection* 42 London: Home Office

Flin, R. (1996) *Sitting in the Hot Seat: leaders and teams for critical incident management* London: John Wiley

Heath, R. and Ryan, M. (1989) 'Public Relations' role in defining corporate social responsibility' *Journal of Mass Media Ethics* 4 (1) 21–38

Hulteng, J. (1981) *Playing It Straight* Chester, Conn.: Globe Pequot Press

Jackson, M. and Janssen, P. (1990) 'Disaster and the Moral Appraisal of Corporate Actions' *International Journal of Mass Emergencies and Disasters* 8 (3)

L'Etang, J. (1996) 'Corporate Responsibility and Public Relations Ethics' in J. L'Etang and M. Pieczka (eds.) *Critical Perspectives in Public Relations* London: International Thomson Business Press

Munn, L. (1997) 'Handling the Media at Dunblane' *Civil Protection* 42 London: Home Office

Pearson, G. (1995) *Integrity in Organizations: an alternative business ethic* London: McGraw Hill

Portway, S. (1995) 'Corporate social responsibility: the case for active stakeholder management' in N. Hart (ed.) *Strategic Public Relations* Basingstoke: Macmillan

Robbins, A. (1991) 'Exercise special: three exercises compared' *Civil Protection* 21 London: Home Office

Seddick, M. (1992) 'Training as a basic factor for disaster preparedness and management' *International Civil Defence Journal* Winter

Seib, P. and Fitzpatrick, K. (1995) *Public Relations Ethics* Orlando, Fl.: Harcourt Brace

INDEX

C

Cabinet Office, 50, 110
Caborn, Richard, 170
care: and sensitivity, 131, 155; customer, 21; legal duty of, 181, 188; of staff, 19; of victims and relatives, 38
cause: of a disaster, 9, 12, 13, 15, 80, 124, 142, 178, 179, 187
CBS, 150
Ceefax, 63
central government. *See* government, central
Central Office of Information (COI), 34, 50, 53, 168, 189, 190, 201, 217–18
Channel 4 News, 209
check lists, 26, 35, 108, 113, 151, 154, 157, 188
chemical industry, the, 10, 215
Chernobyl, 9, 46, 52
Civil Affairs Teams, 93
civil authorities, 51, 52
Civil Contingencies Unit (CCU), 50, 51, 52
clarity: importance of, 108
close up pictures, 42, 44; of identifiable people, 169
codes of conduct, 26
commercial radio. *See* independent local radio (ILR)
commercial television, 64
common factors: of disasters, 11, 48
communication: channels of, 51, 53, 189; failure, 11, 15, 97, 187, 193, 203; inter-agency, 86, 92, 95; planning, 24; political/military, 87; with staff, 18

community: leaders, 104; local, 11, 17, 28, 35, 49, 58, 59, 60, 63, 64, 70, 73, 85, 101, 104, 128
compensation, 20, 143, 145, 169, 170, 179, 212
competitive tendering: by NGOs, 95
complacency, 23
confidentiality, 100; patient, 27
consultation: in plan preparation, 21, 26
co-operation, 109, 189
co-ordination, 24, 47, 109, 162
courtesy: towards the media, 109, 115
cover-up, 24, 104
credibility, 39, 104, 113
crisis. *See also* emergency. *See also* disaster; centre, 194; communication plan, 197; planning, 150, 195
crisis management, 124
criticism, 14, 16, 132, 144, 169, 177, 182, 193
crowd: behaviour, 10; control, 124, 130, 134, 135, 168
Cukurca, 92, 94
culture: corporate, 16; organisational, 86; safety, 15
cuttings libraries, 141, 194

D

Daily Express, 142, 145, 220
Daily Mirror, 132, 136
Daily Post, 128, 133, 138, 150
Daily Star, 134
Dalkon Shield, 212
deadline, 36, 56, 58
Dealing with Disaster, 50
de-briefing, 19, 176, 200